To Connie,
you gladden
many hearts.

RULES OF THE UNIVERSE

Fondly,

Ken Shiovitz

ISBN-13: 978-1532945595
ISBN-10: 1532945590

Website: rulesoftheuniverse.com
Email: ken@rulesoftheuniverse.com

Cover photo: "An Impression of Universe" by the author, uses two objects painted by Cathy Shiovitz. A pulse of light reflects off one object onto the other, while both objects illuminated from another direction by the sun.

Back cover author photo by Tom Hefferan.

Dedication

This book is dedicated to my wife, Cathy, who has lovingly traveled with me and always made sure I knew on which side of the line we were hiking.

Author, right, with Doctoral Advisor, Bill Thompson as appeared in 1974 in Natural History Magazine article, Song of the Bunting.

Preface

Come, let's vacation together. This will be a lot less expensive than a trip to Patagonia or a seat on the Space Shuttle and you'll travel a whole lot farther. We shall start by poking a bug and end up poking the universe. We begin coloring within the lines and eventually flow over some boundaries that appear artificial.

As a lifelong student of behavior, which is a nice name for a tendency to test limits and sometimes catch public humiliation, I've tried hard to learn the norms of society and rules for survival. I even made an honest effort to master the discipline required of science. Eventually, my creative self always seemed to outpace the rigorous approach. I boarded a plane leaving Montreal at the end of my scientific career and heard a fellow passenger say, "You've gotta make a dollar every day." That was as foreign to me as the five-week German course I took to pass the language requirement for my doctoral degree. Indeed, my subsequent career in business faced similar head winds. I was a fine real estate agent with a lot of satisfied folks, but did not have the discipline of a McDonald's to make exactly the same product the same way each time. Survival money was a motivator, but the creative and philosophical self always kicked in whenever I could afford to look up. About 20 years ago, I began to go to Torah discussions and write poetry.

And now, this book has emerged. It reflects the learning curve of how any of us would cry out against perceived injustices of this world, heal, and eventually begin to master an art form. My early poems are rhymey, didactic, and redundant. Eventually they begin to break free and explore the eggs and nests of life's short season. Then they begin to explore the longer seasons before and after one human lifespan. You may find some of the eggs are broken or even rotten. As any good hiker in nature, I hope this will only excite you to peer into the next dense Juniper. Hopefully you will gain a better sense of the greater rules under which we live.

The book leads up to and ends with some stated Rules of the Universe. Like any good model, these are meant to be shot down, modified, rebuilt, and expanded. Thirty five years ago my model for the coding of indigo bunting song was launched. Unfortunately, while certain I could develop it, I lacked adequate time, financing and yes, maybe the ability. Not everyone is a Wright Brother, but perhaps this book will influence you to take your own insights past the late night, inspired-dream stage.

Much of this book is easily understandable, and hopefully you'll often find it aesthetically pleasing. The first section is called "Setting Out," both because we are setting out on our journey together and because it sets out the underlying philosophy of this book in four short epigraphs. The last three epigraphs are the strongest lines of early poems from which they were lifted. The second section, "Rhymes and Passion" contains complete poems from the same 1995-1999 period. Like so many poets, I began writing as a therapeutic reaction to life events. You will find poems inspired by my sudden halt in the scientific study of birdsong. You will experience the lover of science, jilted, with creative juices still flowing, and relief at freedom from its discipline.

Poems of the third section, "Expanding Perspective" from 2000-2007, reflect the exploration of broader styles and subject matter. Poetic elements besides rhythm and rhyme began to appear. The tone poem, "Kitchen Shopping," has been a successful presentation piece that derived from recordings of the song of the indigo bunting, *Passerina cyanea*, at one-quarter speed. It's rhythmic source was recognized only after it was composed. This section forays into descriptions of nature and social thought. It launches recurring themes that explore the essence of peace, war, defense, and survival. In short, this was a period of experimentation and artistic growth.

The fourth section, "Survive and Prevail" 2008-2015, includes many poetic descriptions of efforts to survive and prevail in a world affected by both natural laws, and rules constructed by humans. Some of these efforts are by plants or animals and some by humans. Recurring themes include boundaries, waves, birds, and human perseverance.

In the last section that leads up to the stated "Rules of the Universe," many accepted "Rules of Poetry" get violated. A primary character, Patty, can go forward and backward in time. She is often human, but can be a cosmic entity, such as a planet or a part of a black hole... sometimes simultaneously. She provides alternative perspectives for what we might not otherwise see. She pops up as a sort of intellectual "Where's Waldo?" and the reader is challenged to determine who, when and what she represents. Barry is a much more boring human being, full of the insecurities we all share, who just happens to be the first one to put into words what Patty is trying to make obvious.

Formal training in the science of Ethology, which is Animal Behavior from biological rather than psychological roots, breaks through the surface of many of my poems. So do the fruits of popular reading and professorial / friend discussions in physics, astronomy, and evolution. These are melded together with formal religious training through high school, lay leadership and study as an adult, experience as a public health official, surgical scrub nurse, curator of study skins and bones, tenant, landlord, real estate agent, office managing broker, actor, poetry venue host, and teacher.

With all the unforeseen experiences, I feel satisfied that so far I have had a wonderful life. This attitude probably stems from a secure upbringing, but clearly is because of the unwavering support of my wife, children, and so many family members, colleagues, and friends. There are lots of non-financial events to celebrate in life.

This book is intended for everyone. We're all bound by invisible lines that modify and restrict our potential. Some restrictions are silly and some are invented by people who want to hold you back to suit their own ends. You can get past the discomfort of crossing the wrong line or the right line for the first time. Please, jump in and travel with me toward the far side of knowledge.

Author as Adolf Freitag in the Seattle Jewish Theater Company production of the Last Night of Ballyhoo, by Alfred Uhry in 2012. To right of author: Alice Bridgforth, Trina Gonzales, Lionel McCann, Kathy Hopkins, Fox Matthews, Susan King (seated).

CONTENTS
(poems with asterisk, see Notes p. 156)

4. Survive and Prevail (2008-2015)   83

*See Poem Notes

List of Illustrations

Sculpted Junipers in Front Yard
30 years of artistic pruning, inspired by the style of Jackson Pollock, exemplifies the resilience of nature in the face of human intervention. Top photo by Tom Hefferan.

1

SETTING OUT

1995 - 1999

Sometimes you just have to poke the bug
and see what HAPPENS.

A question unasked is thought not to be.

I shall start with questions that come from songs of birds
and think on those relationships
for which there are no words.

There is no plane to the edge of knowledge, no train.
You have to go on foot.

Soul of Cherry

Edge of Knowledge

A Question Unasked

Vents Are Open

Sculpted Poetic Lamp
"Soul of Cherry" with four sides sculpted from a cherry round that nobody wanted as free wood, apx 1999. Author became attached to the gnarly piece, and brought it in to be interpreted in themes from three early poems.

2

RHYMES AND PASSION

1995 - 1999

Great?

I was supposed to be great.
What ever happened to me,
defined only by mediocrity?

Medium wealth and medium health,
with promise of riches and poverty,
with little skin things, and pills to fight clots,
and pain from whether I exercise or not.

Some glory from sports,
mixed in with the shame,
and brilliant ideas,
along with the inane.

Results from due diligence
include human err's,
and hard won relations
debase from slacked cares.

Adjustments for decades
become lifelong trends,
and moral imperative
for survival bends.

So now I reflect
knowing not how it ends,
I am really quite happy, and
thank goodness for friends!

With Apologies to a Good Man

I'm sorry Doctor Monheimer,
it's me that skinned the skunk
outside your office window.
It really musta stunk.

The temperatures were lofty,
the sun was beating down,
I thought the courtyard empty
until I saw your frown.

They say in time it passes,
so let us call a truce.
Some swear it can be vanquished by
a soak in tomato juice.

This job is rather precious,
stuffing skins and stripping bone.
A museum life is challenging,
so often I'm alone.

"Hello there Mr. Crocodile,
How are your nails today?"
Refilling para-di-chloro-benzene....
Why do they turn away?

Must I really clean out the colony
of beetles that eat the meat,
with spiders in balanced numbers?
I really can't stand the heat.

You mean I forgot to gut it,
pig so bloated now in death?
I'll charge it with my scalpel,
then retreat for cleansing breath.

But where perform the surgery?
None could be unsublimer.
Perhaps in that deserted courtyard,
beneath window of Dr. Monheimer?

Snowy Sidewalk

There is a ten mile sidewalk
completely hid in snow.
It winds to join two study sites,
founded many years ago.

The workers at each study site
kneel together in a crowd.
They remove the snow with thimbles,
of each flake-load they are proud.

Most work the central areas,
few will chance the edge,
for if one misses finding sidewalk
there's scorn of sacrilege.

And far behind most others
one patch of sidewalk really gleams.
Its ultra-proud curator
basks in high esteem.

Dense sites, not overcrowded,
workers regulate their own.
One near an edge is deselected,
one near the rear goes home.

Sometimes the deselected
tear off their winter suits,
and disappear across the snow
wearing nothing but their boots.

But it happens only rarely,
one moves surely to the edge.
"Slow down!" "Watch out!" "Be Careful!"
as if it were real ledge.

Suddenly the one starts running
across the open snow.
crossing unseen sidewalk
far beyond the work-fire's glow.

Returning in the darkness
snowsuit hung again on hook of fact,
yet avoided like the naked ones
who never made it back.

And from the morning thimblers,
a shout of joy is heard,
"We can see a bit of sidewalk.
All together now, forward!"

"The wind must have blown it exposed
in footstep shape," they cry.
"Hey, someone spat on my sidewalk Patch,
I'll see the bastard fry."

Listen to the traveler
even tho' the facts are old,
for there may be another way
and that way may be cold.

Associations*

There is something I divine,
from avian song into my mind,
about the rules that make us tick,
to hit a softball with a stick,
and how the tick precedes the tock,
as measured by tooth on gear of clock,
and how the hands go round and round,
but never can go up or down,
until comes Daylight Savings Day,
the clock must change, but just one way,
for hands jump forward, later back,
but never up nor down, in fact.

Yet serves its function by its rules,
the minute hand knows not its tools,
just moves around that circle face,
and leaves itself no single trace,
but look at hour hand to see,
it moves almost imperceptibly.
Starting at one, minute hand-circle is through,
now hour hand magically is pointing at two.

Alas, My Love! (Of Science)

She stood motionless under the street lamp nearby.
Still beautiful, her surface appearance was rather......granular.
She was hard, granitic, about the size of......a living room.
She had many faces......although not so many as me, I think.

I looked blankly at her foot.
Around it were strewn dried remains of once-beautiful
        flowers and boxes of chocolates.
Also faintly noticeable were plastic bags of
        dried dung.

I greeted her as I had so often done before.
        She said nothing.
        She did nothing.
        It still infuriated me.
        I kicked the dirt once again.

My thoughts turned to our affair.
She had not at first appeared attractive to me.
Later she won me over entirely on the basis of her personality.
I have loved and hated her ever since.

When I loved her most, I knew she loved me too.
Then I accomplished much and was proud of it.
She surely scorned me when I failed.
        I hated her then.

My jealousy of her other suitors was initially intense.
"She loves ME," they would shout.
        I suspect they brought her flowers and chocolate.
With confidence of her love, they rose to dominate me.
How could I deny that she loved them better?
        She has never actually......spoken to me.

Now, by a different path, I again leave her,
    Glancing back toward the faint aroma of fresh flowers,
        so dark and distant,
            but I think I see
                a small cloud of dust.

Vessel With Closing Vents

When I was young, the winds blew right through me,
but I hardly noticed them, since most of my vents were open.
They were more like continuous breezes.
         They did not buffet or press.
             They were part of the background.

Occasionally I grabbed a banana as it flew past, and ate.
    I grew.

My friends also grew.
In fact most grew almost too quickly.
        Some grew taller,
              some grew smarter, and
                   some grew tougher.

I was eating a banana that had recently flown by,
        when I noticed a friend holding *two* bananas.
"Hey, how'd you get so lucky to grab two bananas?" I shouted.
He answered, "Closed a vent last night and one flew in
        and hit it on the way out."
"Oh," I mumbled,
        not quite knowing what to do with
           such a radical concept.

Most of my friends were up to their knees in bananas
        before I tried closing my first vent.
They were laughing at me of course.
        This was well before any
           had died of over-ingestion.

I was slower, shorter, and more boring than anyone
        except the girl who was born
           with a vent deficiency.
Believe me, it does not help one's self-image
        to be the slowest one to
           begin closing vents.

Now I am older.
Now most of my vents are closed.

Now many of my playmates are
dead, senile, or pitiful.

I still hope to create,
but the winds are howling.
The pressure inside is immense.

New matter can hardly blow in against the gradient.
Old matter is eliminated by chance,
as it flows
near one of the few open vents left.

The pressure grows painful.
I have two choices:
eat faster
open some vents.
Open too many vents and bingo, senility!
Eat too much and you get heart disease.
I think I will just go
play softball.

In a Bathtub

I sit in a bathtub
    floating free
        with mind and body.

Locked, not free!
    I am tied pole-tight to my predecessors,
        my followers.

I sit in a bathtub so my progeny can sit in a bathtub,
    so theirs can sit in a bathtub,
in a bathtub,
    in the future equivalent of a bathtub.

Dad sat in a bathtub,
    grandpa sat in a bathtub,
        cave dad sat in a pool of water.

I hear the screams of my great aunts,
distant past relatives.
    They grunted so I can sit in a bathtub.

I scan bathroom ceiling, tile walls, soap dish.
    I see my belly, legs, toes.
I wiggle my toes; push soap in the soap dish.
    Humans gave me the walls, my toes, soap dish.
I flex sexual muscles.
    I will give later humans their toes,
        their soap dish.

Contribute and die!
    We live to add in a direction that is clearly discernible.
Contribute to the pool of humans.
    Contribute to the pool of human knowledge.

We cannot resist the direction.
    Such efforts only get in the way of others.

Or there will be no bathtub,
    there will be no soap dish,
        there will be no collection of useful thoughts.

Yo-Yo*

Shimmering iridescent plaything,
guardian of cosmic truth,
mindless, repetitious pastime,
unlock your secrets of matter-time.

Fling out then catch tiny planetoid,
Force measured true by silken thread,
Big Bang propels forth thy Duncan,
Black Hole, my hand in gravity, awaits.

"Loop-the-Loop" and "Around-the-World,"
My hand, thy fate awaits,
"Walk-the-Doggie" then "Rock-the-Cradle,"
Black Hole awaits, yet unaware.

Now atoms blend and join from heat,
while moving outward Duncan still,
then tiny cells form organ groups,
silken thread now a tad long.

And thread stretches on 'til out of sight,
tracked yet by telescope.
Last earthly glimpse shows ears and feet,
                    and thumb on nose to all.

Another Useless Poem

One more useless poem,
    delivered through encephalic sphincter
        of yet one more useless poet.

Meaningless drivel of analogy and simile,
    like digital exploration of Roget's Thesaurus,
        by nearsighted, finger-amputated, wheelchair philosopher.

Familiar~droning~rhythmic~intonation,
    of faceless~replaceable~National~Public~Radio~voices,
        eliciting~visual~images~of farm tractors~and~hands,
           gnarly~hands,
           knobby~sinewy~veiny~ life-distorted ~hands.

Sappy, awestruck, spirit-sopped revelations,
    endlessly envisaged hallucinogenic impressions,
          about the Moon,
          about the Great Blue Heron,
          about the Moon.

Wine-soaked street poet and
    award-soaked postdoctoral academic poet,
          cowboy poet,
          child poet,
          urban-butch, imminent-death, reflective poet.

Nothing meaningful to say,
    nothing novel except a different mind and mouth,

nothing but a
          different perspective.

Backyard Waterfall and Pond
Under-gravel filtered water is pumped to top of rockery and back
through waterfall at upper left, through a small settling pond, then
under a rock slab back into the pond. Tunnel and overhanging rocks
provide protection for the fish.

Backyard Bridge
"A Peaceful Crossing to a Quiet Place." Author pegged out curved
supports for months, only to have them straighten up when re-
leased. Curve maintained by spacers over 2 X 4s. Calligraphy by
Cathy Shiovitz.

3

EXPANDING PERSPECTIVE

2000 - 2007

Transfer Station

Purple leaves stubborn-clung to Maple,
crinkled upward pointing lobes,
vein-protruding survivor hands,
malformed, yet recognizable in prayer.

In contrast, bare lay ancient Ginkgo,
disloyal yellow fans abandoned,
dumped entire in two days time,
blown vacant from mounded base of trunk.

Driving in late autumn stirs the poet,
draws attention to nature's color,
bathes the soul in warmth unseasonable,
blurs all sense of things abnormal.

No traffic except garbage truck in left-hand lane,
permits full sense of autumn bounty,
turning right across my path.
Delight-to-doom takes but an instant.

The insect body, I have been taught,
from early age in Science class,
has three wee parts that work in tandem,
the head, thorax, and abdomen.

An instant's glimpse of first the head,
shining bright from chitin shell,
predator turning toward its prey,
dwarfing inevitable morsel of fate.

Now thorax and abdomen loom above,
chitin shell so clearly iron,
lever-legs protrude obliquely,
cephlo-thorax will smash my head.

I always thought that I was Maple,
clinging hard for life's addendum.
Never would I quit and drop,
like Ginkgo, aboriginally young.

Soft lawn beyond feelers fatal,
ignore firm curb, just miss that pole.
Suddenly, sweet driveway beckons,
outstretched arms draw love embrace.

Miracles endure but moments,
sweet scent of spring in autumn's turn,
Summer warmth in displaced season,
life's full senses simultaneously sung.

Truck was turning into alley.
No miracle, just events that were.
I still said prayer of grateful thanking,
hugged secretaries when I arrived.

Old Hat

It was just an old hat,
      worn by summer hair,
      worn by winter wind,
just an old worn hat,
      nothing noble,
      nothing natty,
except maybe......
....for a sewn cloth label.
"New York Hat and Cap,"
      very classy label,
      very classy Manhattan apartment,
two classmates in adjoining bedroom,
      beckoning gape of door ajar,
      beckoning white brassiered bounty.
Would it were worth the price of indulgence!
.....for a trace of stain, where band meets brim.
non-greasy formula SPF 45 with Aloe Vera,
      prevents proliferation of undisciplined dermis.
      proboscis paled from local anesthetic,
dare to flick just one eye open?
      yawning purple of uncooked meat,
      yellow-red of fringe and fold.
Would spider-web thin threads hold firm?
.....for a few furtive follicles sustaining pigment.
Behold the color of color, the presence of presence,
      ghost enhancing visage of gray,
      gas-filled vacuoles promoting invisibility!
Grampa's beard was flaming forceful,
      strands of red appeared in mine,
      strands of brown and black and blond.
Would that the only loss were body heat!
.....for one small stitch above the brim,
one stitch to hold material fold in place,
      one stitch in time,
      one snap release from regimen and rule.
Unsnapped the old blue cap defined chauffeur.
      Cap of dunce, and grad, and fool,
    Coolie hat, Arabian kaffiyeh,
Would that I still could wear them all!

Missed

1.
Cloudy gray mist, nearly impervious
to yellow fog-lights, only partially covered
the, *pick whom you follow*, smelling
like the taste of metal, until
counter-measures of whipped cream and
three flavors of candied syrup were applied.

2.
Hidden inside an abandoned mine car,
edges flaking rust alongside an old shovel,
Pick breathed imperceptibly to avoid detection.
Above the mine, a drab bar-feathered owl, moaned
"*Whoooooooom*," subtly lowering amplitude at the finish.
Ripe with rotting grasses, in field below mine's gape,
You, white with woolen sheen, grazed nervously.

3.
Directly before the blue-gray of a basalt pillar, stood
Mohandas Gandhi, Adolf Hitler, Jimmy Carter, and Jessie James.
Each called out "*Follow* Me," repeatedly, in enticing voices.
So the people all followed Adolf, because
he was handing out free T-shirts that read,
"Third Reich Rocks."

Kitchen Shopping*

Tong.

Tonnng....
Tonnng....
Whisk!
Waffle, Waffle,
Whisk!

Tonnng....
Tonnng....
Whisk!

Buffet, Buffet, Buffet.
Goblet, Coaster,
Whisk!

Trivet.
Trivet.
Goblet, Coaster,
Whisk!

Trivet.
Trivet.
Buffet, Dinnerware.
Buffet, Dinnerware.

Popover! Popover!
Goblet, Coaster,
Whisk!

Dinnerware.
Dinnerware.
Goblet, Coaster,
Whisk!

Tureen....
Tureen....
Buffet, Dinnerware.

Tureen....
Tureen....
Goblet, Coaster,
Whisk!

Whisk!
Whisk!
Mincer, Coaster,
Whisk!

Whisk!
Tureen, Whisk!
Whisk!
Tureen.
Tonnng....
Tonnng....
Tonnng....

Whisk!

Boundaries

The membrane of cell,
when viewed through a 'scope,
surrounds it entire
in sealed envelope.

'Though many come begging
for entry inside,
permeability limits,
through fat and peptide.

While freedom and safety
thrive inside of border,
they can't be maintained
without internal order.

For membrane has pores
that penetrate deep,
lined with more membranes,
that security keep.

So cellular commerce
survives untrodden,
from virus or anthrax,
or Osama bin Laden.

Shadows

The night he retired, we drank dark beer.
He bought.
Soft visage, balding pate,
he did not look like a killer.
As so well I knew him, by soul,
a mist was he, by deed.

Neither threatening in height,
nor square of shoulder, I saw
no Soldier.
He looked woolen, like your grandfather,
or in black pajamas and huge Turkish mustache,
like your Mediterranean grandfather.

How could I sit so near his shadow,
I tangible, while he a spook?
How could I even weigh his stature,
a Hero,
six times wounded without tribute,
returning home without a story?

To measure is but to be a male,
to watch every war movie made,
absorb every action documentary,
behold every battle photograph,
and wonder:
can Warrior legs be grafted onto mine?

While friend was fixed behind a wall,
and shatter-spatter filled his ears,
I dove behind a Graduate School deferment,
with dread of death no less real,
drawing fire from draft board head,
Mad Mary.

Her massive body equaled four of mine, she
had saluted and buried three soldier husbands,
thought, "Thus would grieve every mother and wife,"
bellowed, "Graduate students must grovel in the dust."
Behind my wall in the waiting room,
I hunched,
    paralyzed.

The Fox

Sweet spring wetness mats fur of fox into drippy pyramids,
while morning mist still fogs newly wakened eyes, and spray,
shaken dog-style from back, smacks upon mossy trunks.

Canid sinus encounters hungry scent, fresh of hare and vole,
competing with full aching aroma of female-in-heat.
Lured by each, *Vulpes fulva* tarries in indecision.

Sudden soft crunch of sodden wood chip reaches erect ears,
rabbit bolts from rotten cedar log in rapid fright,
fox without hesitation cuts angle of pursuit.

The end is stereotyped; a script prewritten over eons:
first jaws lock on anything, knocking prey askew,
next jaws clamp on neck...a jerk, a snap....
and breakfast is served.

Far away, that same night, another fox is mulling,
weighing pain, assessing aches, hungering, then
calmly views the hundred heads about him, and calls out, "Fire!"

Overlooked in crowded theatre, trampled toddler had
loved the zoo, understood little of behaviors consummatory,
or where the eons have
left us wild.

The Fall

It hovered above the hungering hole, pendulant,
like deadened hammerhead of steel sledge,
one massive cylinder of bundled cellulose,
supported by single perpendicular side root, the
brown and scaly beached carp, wrapped
in dried, distorted rectangles, with turned-up edges,
holding aloft a mass ten times its diameter,
a thousand times its weight.

For twenty-five summers, solid Engelmann Spruce, while
grasping ever deeply into highland sands, they uplifted
from ocean bottom a millennium before, and still without
anchoring boulder or even toehold of clay, consistently had
repelled hostile downpours of hail and of rain.
bent before storm winds blowing in off the water,
distributed forces through trunk base to roots, as it
grew massive and strong.

Now it just hung there, defiant and threatening,
a face absent features, no eyebrow, beard, nor hair,
nose, lips, and ears lopped off by a chainsaw,
thirty feet of former trunk neatly stacked in rounds,
every side root, save one, shaved close to the stump,
huge taproot, dissected free from loose sand, and
though clinging to life by mere technicality, still it
flaunted a bone crushing weight.

But slow! Its final moments engender quiet respect,
distinct from fear of digging beneath wooden wrath,
apart from professional pride of engineer in
determining depth and slope of descent,
contrasting with continuous attack of circulating saw
teeth tearing tenaciously at naked nape of neck,
rather, solemn silence shrouds, as final heave sends
sliding stump of spruce to rest.

Shaving Cream

Silken foamy flow of soft smooth whiteness whooshes
free from compact confines of cylindrical armory,
pouring forth wave after wave of bubbly defense,
to save my skin, to save my face.

Later it will seem strange that I even had that can of shaving cream,
bearded full for thirty consecutive summers,
trimming irregularly by scissors or electric clipper,
bare-faced but for four more years.

Dad had instructed me early in the timeless mantra of manhood:
"The wetter the shave, the better the shave."
He was referring to use of the blade, for electric razors desire dry skin,
but blades glide briskly in bubbles of soap or shaving cream.

Wetter is better also in the baking heat of summer at Camp Tamarack,
where relief is measured by time spent floating upon the dark green
lake,
as far as possible from the continuous shrieking of campers,
and moments of independent solitude are treasured, but always no-
ticed.

Like typical human societies, hierarchical in status and possessions,
access to camp watercraft had followed strict traditions.
No mere rowboat, or even swift canoe, I had trembled visibly as was
passed to me
from last year's Assistant Dorm Head, use of the only camp sailboat.

This slab of white Styrofoam came complete with centerboard and
sail,
the mast embedded in a cavity of concrete block, tied aboard with
rope.
Working the tiller by trial and error, I soon learned to cut the lapping
waves,
gliding across wet expanses, leasing freedom at a price.

Those eyes I felt, the force to encounter, the order to peck,
came not from the society I knew, of campers and counselors and
dorm heads,
but from the other society at hand, of mowers and maintenance and

locals,
the hired townies, the Hartland Boys.

A year earlier, in 1964, at the Hartland General Store and Gas Station,
with a car-full of camp staff, we had waited for 15 minutes by the
pump,
the gas attendant in a porch chair, sitting, rocking, smirking, just
watching us.
"It is because of me," said a counselor, whom I had forgotten was
black.

I did not fear the Hartland Boys, even though one was huge,
and all could operate motorized farm implements.
They just were not a part of camp society,
and they did not seem particularly bright.

Yet one day they had made their intentions clear, using the prized sail-
boat as a raft,
remorselessly removing cement block and mast,
showing no regard for camp traditions of property rights, and
ignoring all attempts to enlighten them in this matter, except the in-
voking of authority.

At summer camp, rumors of intended revenge shortly precede the
actual event,
permitting time for concern and mental preparation.
Far too late for a course in martial arts or construction of anti-tractor
defenses,
survival in summer camp, hinges only upon your history and your
head.

My real training consisted of growing up the second of four brothers,
wrestling for fun and food,
learning moves and scams by observation and reflex,
standing regularly in the corner as punishment, well deserved...

When the lights suddenly went out, I was prepared.
Already the scam was part of the worldly knowledge of camp males:

sneak quietly into utility area of dorm, after campers are asleep,
loosen main fuse on moonless night, attack sleeping victim in total
blackness.

In instant reaction, I slipped from my cot, and turned it noiselessly on its side.
Behind this barrier, I armed myself with the weapons at hand:
Right-Guard Deodorant spray in left hand,
Bristol-Meyers Foamy Shaving Cream in the right.

The battle itself was acute and decisive.
When blind contact with the reoriented cot evoked a murmur of surprise, I opened fire.
Holding off the left flank with Right-Guard, I aimed shaving cream for the head area.
It spurted forth valiantly, volley after volley, mound upon foamy mound.

"That's enough," I heard a voice say in surrender. "I give up."
The face, not yet seen, was obscured by drippy white sheets of lather.
I connected the body hulk and voice to one of the Hartland Boys.
His slim friend stooped quietly nearby, looking humble.

The hulky guy, by coincidence, had the same name as my brother, Bill.
He and his quiet friend, Ray, turned out to be pretty sincere and gentle fellows.
I cannot remember if we shared the sailboat for the rest of the summer.
It just no longer mattered.

Sensory Overload (9/11/2001)

Soft, as a stick skewers silent marshmallow,
firm as false-faith in concrete, now powder,
hot, as a girder glows orange-yellow, sparking,
cold as a curse, cutting fouled fall air.

Soft, as an airplane probes pulp of stiff tower,
firm as a nation's resolve to recover,
hot as a hound's breath in relentless pursuit,
cold as pure justice, delivered when due.

Mr. Chairman

Certainly, the bronze metallic chair was solidly built,
legs and struts fashioned from stout tubes of aluminum,
flattened from press, and punctured by diamond-tipped steel bit,
firmly bolted through inch long welds to lock-washer rigidity.

He had never thought of it as anything but reliable furniture,
capable of holding an ample dinner guest, without quavering,
part of a set of four, surrounding the simple brown Formica table,
arrayed symmetrically beneath a single suspended light bulb.

Much later he would recline into black leather and mahogany,
facing executives, with formal suit jacket and tightly knotted tie,
enjoying selected comforts at the cost of lost dreams,
retracing forest pathways, while crossing city streets.

He recalled that the bronze metallic chair was a hand-me-down,
donated incidentally from parental storage to hopeful newlyweds,
transported nearly seven hundred miles by professional van,
sealed through customs, and bound for a city where they call it a siege.

But on the return trip, they had silently driven a rental truck,
with only three aluminum chairs stowed insecurely inside.
He remembered how the businessmen spoke a foreign language,
"You've got to make a dollar every day," they laughed.

Before he had learned to replace one dream with another,
he serenely spent their savings to complete his work,
and then one sweaty summer evening, in isotonic slow motion,
he pressed one formerly functional bronze metallic chair into a pan-
cake.

Water

Resistant moisture rounds renewed into droplets,
runs wandering over retardant rock,
released, rolls from rim edge:

Drip,
Dart,
Dab Dip,
Dig Dirt,
Dim Dark,
Drop.

Tapping tinkle triple-times plinking tour in groove,
takes twinkle-troop topping time-etched terrace,
twists rivulet in pickled kink.

Plops past pepper spatter,
prepares plush passionate push,
precipitately passes porous pleasure pressure,
polishing always.

Soushes through smattering of shallow sluices,
sending standing soldier shafts of sophism,
surging silently along chosen channels,
stutter-foams across steeper stepping-stones.

Flowing farther, following fastidiously, flagging fastness,
foolish fancies force fallible fortune, further fantasy,
feinting falsehoods forbear in face of factual comfort,
slows its surging fascist philosophy to power of flood.

Whole wide wandering waters wallow in shallow expanse,
wasting warrior waltzes slowly over deeper deposits of detritus,
white caps flash and disappear above withering weight of destiny.

Meandering moribund multitude in muted imaginary motion,
magnetically meets massive stationary mere,
and in final muddy termination, just
mires.

Harmony

Slough no tear for callus worn
from hand that shields the wind,
nor mourn the stinger neatly torn
from queen's responsive kin.

Slice living stalk beneath plump germ,
without a moment's notice,
and crush the elongated worm,
'neath your lover's writhing pelvis.

Marvel at the blowfly's wing,
but keep it from your fodder.
Listen to the poet sing,
but keep him from your daughter.

For human bonds, learned or innate,
cold nature must resist,
and peace is but a balanced state,
of powers harmonious.

Flyway

A mid-May morning dawns so cool that breath clouds
hang expectant, then slowly vaporize, where soon
hot, audible pants of exhalation will accompany
honored scramble through mixed habitat,
in absolute silence, save for a deafening single
lap of waves and song of ten thousand birds.

Wrapped in a swarm of flitting feathers, surreal peninsula,
Point Pelee, Ontario, slices southward into Lake Erie,
implores flapping passes from Pelee Island, while siphoning
weary scattered stragglers, spread wide above white-capped waters,
to safety of tree-belted tarmac, just beyond the grayish ribbon
from fish carcasses rotting on sands of the broadening beach.

Bearing the bravado of sculpted models at Malibu,
perching migrants return to Pelee in vibrating flocks,
males in full breeding coloration and aggressiveness,
flaunting strength and song upon exposed tree tips,
fencing, fighting, flying from forest limbs, displaying
in a passionate swirl of lust and hate and hope and love.

It is the finest hour of Madison Avenue,
full scale advertising in advance, before
house building or land purchase, before
territories are reached and secured, before
hidden nests are woven between four stalks of goldenrod,
even before the resting and reading up of old newspapers.

Pelee is a number on the face of a clock, a checkpoint in time,
a balance sheet for hours of daylight, for insects ingested,
for the days it takes to complete a journey, the days
for searching out home and mate, and reaffirming identity,
days for fattening, and nesting, and raising young,
a reminder of why the long dangerous trek is ever necessary.

Some say that autumn at Pelee is beautiful, but quiet;
absent are the hundreds of bird watchers and spiritualists....
A few of the observed thousands prepare for the return hop,
but they are nearly silent, replenishing energy spent,
last remnants of small groups of drab new hatchlings
and unfulfilled parents turning back in hope of renewal.

Out of Time

Scarcely rippling waters shimmer
about the basal bark of flooded forest
of leggy, randomly spaced Sugar Maples,
nearly identical in lamp pole girth and length,
lichen encrusted trunks stretching to treetops,
aging in concert then frozen in time.

Noonday light filters through leafless branches,
defining shadowy circles of lofty heron nests,
large clumps of woven sticks with sedge grass linings,
casting complex patterns of glint and dark reflection
upon the soothing surface of running clear shallows,
which seep underground deeply to smother living roots.

Built slightly downstream, a massive beaver dam
shamelessly deflects the smallest of rivulets
by complex blockage of interlacing logs and branches,
lined and filled with softly sloping mound of sand,
scooped with paddle tail and packed pertly in place,
sends water wandering among growing stands of hardwoods.

Far above the gently perking artificial pond,
embedded in canopy, nearly level with nesting herons,
leafy camouflage hides a gray, weathered-wood blind,
secured by lag bolts to four clustered maple trunks,
swaying floor penetrated by rusty-hinged trap door,
above access ladder of shaky stakes nailed centrally.

Barely beyond the fringing shore-muck floats a rowboat,
shallow in draft, with wooden hull unpainted and worn,
long oars removed from locks for shoving off from land
with enough force to glide between nearest emergent trunks,
pushing at them to steer and power the last few boat lengths
before reaching the bottom rung of that unsturdy ladder.

An arm, thrust out from the boat, meets a mossy trunk,
which, internally rotten throughout its 40 foot height,
instantly falls in almost equal two foot segments,
fan-folding to smack the waters in a single splash,
like a perfect Olympic swan dive,
startling the visitor with suddenness and ensuing silence.

The visitor watches as two experienced observers
clamber up the slatted ladder and, holding with one hand,
flip opened the hatch, to haul their bodies through the hole....
but, despite desire to watch the wing thrust of descending heron,
the leggy grasp of claw onto arched edge of gape-filled nest, and
the slither of regurgitated fish inside funnel bill of pimply young,
he will simply freeze upon the third slat of the ladder.

Passing Freedom

For Cells, Gels, and Gerald Pollack

Driving ferociously down the urban freeway,
we pass plodding carloads of capitulated passengers,
daydreaming of distant vacations, encapsulated,
barely conscious of speed limits and lurking patrol cars.

They are marking their way to work or to visit mother,
changing lanes in a carefully controlled manner,
neither travelling too fast nor noticeably lagging traffic,
proud of the right to be free, while driving in preformed grooves.

As therapy, the act of speeding has its drawbacks,
evidenced dramatically by the destroyed sports car,
former shiny red Italian symbol of individuality,
now walnut, cracked open around unforgiving lamppost.

Our car slows to conform, with the inevitability of a sneeze,
while inside, insecure opinions flip between two
conformational states:
that enduring peace arises only from political compromise, and
that unchecked, people have the capacity to continue killing, even millions.

Speeding up, the armor of our SUV steels support
for another theory:
that with burglar alarm and rod-buttressed doors,
frame and roll bars,
one would need a tremendous amount of energy
to really threaten us,
but as we hit 94, we pass a smashed Ford Explorer on the shoulder of
the road.

Again, our car slows to conform, plodding along tired tread marks,
providing no citadel or stone walled storehouse, no Maginot Line,
frankly defining the face of our freedom by the forces of nature:
we are water molecules locked in the gel of wondrous cytoplasm.

And like the cell, we depend for security and survival
on phase transitions,

changes that permit free movement, until those very movements
cause change,
dramatically returning to configurations that exclude and attract
selectively:
a never-ending cycle of the feather and the sword.

Insight

I used to think that beard trims were there to
mark major events in human existence, then
I strongly suspected that my heart medicine,
popped daily in the form of a dour white pill,
counted the remaining mornings of my life,
but after much impatience with such false indicators,
I have now come to believe
it is the coffee filters.

Weir

Within the weir of woven willow branches,
frantic salmon boil beneath frothing waters,
like live-trapped raccoon gnashing at steel mesh,
wildly probing lattice seams, but completely wired in.

Long ago, weird-looking fish with fleshy-lobed fins,
struggled from diminished streams onto flats of mud,
working stiff legged, like elongated circus stilt walkers,
budding lobes bagged off where esophagus swallowed air.

Now we are people, sucking lungs full of oxygen,
clawing at networks of withering rainforests,
like inmates behind clammy walls of iron and rock,
scratching with fingernails to wear at grains of mortar.

We cook with wares of pottery and Pyrex glass,
hoping to extend survival beyond pre-ordained limits,
like lucky salmon, tail-flung above fallen tree limbs,
to add the smallest increment to life, but oh so weary.

I Ain't Nobody's Food

Just keep your distance until I get to know you a little better,
me over here, and you over there…way over there,
and maybe I'll tell you why it is
that I'm not looking to live forever.

Now I suppose you are tending toward living as long as you can,
so I'm thinking too…but that don't mean to come any closer,
then maybe I'll tell you a coupla methods that
you definitely don't want to try.

First, don't be the seventeen-year locust and sleep your life away.
Sure you spread out the pain…don't be coming any closer,
but you feel nothing except a good orgasm or two,
then you just rot up and melt away.

Don't be the elephant or the tortoise and get huge and slow, neither,
Somebody will notice…keep your slow ass behind that line,
and your hollowed-out feet will be made into ashtrays,
leave the rest of you for the vultures.

Mostly, don't expect science or progress to come to the rescue.
New eyeglasses maybe, but…back, back, I ain't your grocery store.
They can fix your rotten genes and heal you, and maybe
you're going to live for a very long time.

But think about my next-door neighbor Maxine, pushing that baby
carriage out of high school,
Young mother, young grandmother…keep that saliva in your mouth
and listen,
Maxine's baby had a baby about the same time I did.
Lost one whole generation before I turned thirty.

Now I figure, the way bacteria and viruses get resistance,
dying is a just way of getting stronger…slow down, I ain't finished
speaking.
So, Maxine's family is way more evolved than mine,
and I can only catch up by dying.

Now the real tragedy comes if science and progress keep me alive
forever.

Then I become food for Maxine's kin...you kind of bear her a resem-
blance.
They would keep me as some sort of cow, budding off regenerated
arms for supper.
But hell, I ain't gonna be nobody's food.

Oscillations

Stark August sun bleaches contrast from a San Diego beach,
nearly concealing jellied secrets, scattered over baking sands,
each sporting suction-cupped tentacles, speckled with silicates:
fifty tons of fusiform squids silently rotting after a summer storm.

Barely moving amongst the squid, irregularly arrayed masses of
bending human bodies, bloated from French fries and bologna,
mounds of rolling reddened skin in skimpy bathing suits,
toss decomposing mollusks into buckets of stinking slime.

The stench reaches even to an ancient gray shack upon the cliff,
where an old man makes kissing sounds with his toothless mouth,
watches sleek Western Gulls hover above rotund beach walkers,
thinks saline droplets, excreted from bill glands, are really tears.

Occasionally a gull swoops low between girthy laborers,
grabs a choice looking corpse, and returns to the cliff ledge, where
gaping downy balls, newly hatched from roll-resistant eggs with
one enormous end, grasp eagerly at the red spot of a parental bill.

Having watched the cyclical nature of cliff-life for many years,
the old man knows the outcome of this season in advance,
like dependency of Snowy Owl upon the Arctic Hare, that
without free access to rotting squid, the gull population will suffer.

He also knows that nature has a knack for unceasing compensation,
that massive orders of fried potatoes supply enough blubber to rival
an Orca,
that the gulls are plunging ever closer to pluck at human-tossed mor-
sels,
and that one day, the slop buckets will be overturned.

Louise

Lightly her fragile frame greeted an angular chair,
that surrounded narrow soft arms,
hands silently folded about her hanky,
nestled in the remnant of a life-nurturing lap.

Despite sightless eyes, her face inclined upwards,
slightly cocked in an aspect of attention,
upper torso keeping dignified posture,
she still asserted a forceful presence.

One respected especially her voice,
whispered as ninety-four years surely necessitated,
yet rigorously proper in syntax and inflection,
never failing the former teacher of History.

Nor were her instincts for truth diminished,
as divined instantly by anyone standing before her,
regardless of education or social stature, thinking
how her students must have quaked.

Patiently she listened to a poem about harmony,
remained austere or laughed where appropriate,
acknowledged the cynical summary of physical truths,
        then gently reminded: we cannot live without hope.

The Return

Leah Pinsky remembered how happiness happened,
in the mornings when she and younger sister Miriam,
had brushed each other's long brunette locks,
forcing strangers and family friends alike,
to pause and ponder which pair of milk chocolate eyes
and sable soft cheeks belonged to the prettier sibling.

She remembered laughter in the family house in Minsk,
a stately hewn basalt mansion right on Lotz Boulevard,
where their father was an important community leader,
their gentle mother, socially prominent and proud,
Leah and Miriam attracting hoards of hopeful lovers,
when they were known collectively as the Minsky Pinskys.

After that time, when the family had both money and hope,
most of their wealth would be stolen or spent on bribes,
an eroding shield fronting the unceasing hate of fascism,
until Mr. Pinsky lost both his position and his freedom,
and Leah spent most of her stockpile of hope on Miriam,
until one day even that account was completely depleted.

Leah had consoled Miriam when the furniture vanished,
lovingly shielded her when they were herded onto trains,
sang quietly to her after they were stripped and raped,
pretended with her that their terrible jobs were secure,
shearing the hair from the doomed at Sobibor,
but there was never any happiness to replenish hope.

And finally, they were going home, she and Miriam, together,
among the few who survived escape from a camp,
hiding cold and hungry until the Allies resurrected color,
the two emaciated Pinskys trudged all the way to Minsk,
across the pock-holed wooden bridge onto Lotz Boulevard,
standing to face the hewn basalt mansion of family history.

For two hundred years, Pinskys had lived in that part of Poland,
the last 75, in that very house, which great-grandfather had built,
which Miriam approached too rapidly, weeping, "My home!"
She recognized the local trainmaster, but ignored his warning,
"This is our home now. Go back to where you came from."
Leah held Miriam as her last essence seeped from the gunshot wound.

So Leah found home in the land where she came from,
where relatives had lived continuously for thousands of years,
after the British had stopped her ship and returned her to a camp,
where she had learned about the other side of a shotgun,
where she once again heard, "This is our home now.
Go back to where you came from," which she ignored.

Winter at the Zoo

It is winter at the zoo,
The Tiger paces its cage,
a Camel snorts snowflakes off its nostrils,
and Orangutans huddle in corners.

Outside, a mother and gleeful child
run into the Nocturnal House,
momentarily leaving Dad lost in thought,
before he remembers the need for family and warmth.

Inside, their eyes adjust to the darkness,
see a Kinkajou race - then freeze,
locate the measured motion of a Loris,
find Fruit Bats hanging from branches.

Mother and child marvel at these revelations,
but Dad has again become the zoologist,
thinking about his unproven scientific theory,
that he had to leave behind like the outside light.

He knows he is a Fruit Bat,
hanging from a branch of knowledge,
cloaked in darkness,
on a tree that might not even exist.

Chicken Scratch for Henry

Henry Fowler began avoiding political disputes,
those benumbing promotions of fixed opinion,
such as, holding that survival is threatened only
by the fascist at home, or only by the fascist abroad.

Since he was unemployed and quite broke,
Henry could care less who controlled foreign petrol,
or how multimillionaires mugged the public,
as long as they did not select him to help settle a matter.

Unsullied by petty ambitions beyond remaining alive,
apathy served Henry for as long as he had nothing to lose,
until one day, blind fortune feathered Henry's future with
inheritance of the Plucky Lady, Egg and Chicken Farm.

Henry soon began to admire hens above all other animals,
resulting neither from fluffy fetish, nor errant imprinting experience,
but rather, out of true respect for chicken society.
He much preferred minor pecking episodes
to human misbehavior.

What struck Henry most about hens was impossible to pick:
how they permit you to rapidly grab them up by the beak, or
how quickly they forget and entirely forgive the observed
executioner,
proffering their own unfertilized ova in perfect obeisance.

Almost imperceptibly, Henry began his impending surrender,
for after only one month, he stopped treating hens like objects,
patched drafty cracks in the coop, installed ergonomic perches, and
spent his last profits to raise poultry pleasantry to the highest priority.

Once again broke, Henry could not buck the beckoning tide,
but tightened the buckle of his belt, and mocking his squandered luck,
blandly submitted: if only he had some bucks, some bucks,
some buck, buck, buck.

Pin Wheel

Glint.
Glint to dark.
Glint to dark, yellow dots and red.

Tones of gray meet yellow-red.
Growing lines, increasing speed,
spiral stripes of color blend.

Silver-orange moves air so light,
races 'round as pressure mounts,
blows cicada's vibrant call.

Higher hum with shining flow,
ragged hum now falling low,
ripping loose in glory search.

Flying pin from straw and wheel
launches flight of fading dream,
fins unfurled flap futilely.

Getting Dressed

Today I pick the green shirt,
reject the orange plaid,
because it might seem too cheery,
and the deep blue, too apologetic.

It is so early to stiffen in fear,
stomach empty, save toss of coffee,
no morning workout,
no leisurely bath,
like a soldier stumbling from his tent,
gun in hand,
looking stunned,
nearly shooting without a target.
Still, I do not curse the phone call,
intrusive, like the alarm clock buzz
that shatters an erotic dream,
pitiless, yet inevitable.

Fumbling with buttons,
I explore minds not my own,
and paint scenarios of emotion,
applying hue of mood
to clothing I must wear,
perhaps today evoking
a match in mental fabric
to rival the day I walked summer fields
with a farmer outside Duvall,
who spoke nothing while I talked,
then looked me over slowly,
gradually became animated,
and finally said,
"You are wearing
the same shirt as me."

Natrix Water Snake

Black Snake
blocks
rural road,
suddenly
squirted
from fringe,
across path of
plodding car,
flashes above
compacted sand,
then disappears
into dense foliage,
fringe abutting stream,
so clear and musical,
free of surface oils,
of runoff from
human sources,
instead open
view port,
upon
daily routine
of minnow,
tiny Shiner
startled
from feeding,
posture faced
into current,
maintaining
exact distance
from branch,
submerged
long enough
for algae,
grown into
telltale strings
from current,
to provide
hiding cover,
except

Natrix
Water Snake
awaits,
just on
other side
of slivery
shadow,
perhaps by
serendipity,
more likely
search image
and patience,
instantly
springing
beneath branch,
emerging
retracted
with jaws
jammed full,
body and tail
of shiner
protruding,
then disappearing
into swollen lump,
just behind head
of sated *Natrix*,
sending guilty
shutter through
witness,
although
familiar
with natural
processes,
reminded
of that moment
two years before,
when four foot
Massasauga
Rattler
had slithered
from bog....
to cross

where
they had
hiked,
and the

eternal

instant

before he

could expel,

"Freeze!"

Uncle Henry

His soft hands cradle my wounded spirit,
to heal before I even know it is sore.
For, as long as I live, Uncle Henry is here,
listening intently to the words I speak,
relating my troubles to the broader world,
where everyone experiences disillusionment,
but only some of the strong survive.

Henry is eternally interested in every aspect of nature,
quietly pointing out fish habitats in his little stream
that pours under-fence from the pond of his neighbor,
as he sucks on his pipe,
observing, hearing
every call of every distressed creature,
that crosses his path.

Once I visited Henry before a patient had departed
from the comfortable couch in his office,
a converted family room of the large split-entry home,
where Dr. Henry the Psychoanalyst sat in silence,
sharing indescribable sensory experiences
with another walking capsule,
surface serene as the neighbor's pond.

Henry must have been about 15 years old,
when he watched his neighbors fall exhausted,
and strangers herded past him
emerged again as ashes from the nearby stacks,
when his parents and siblings were torn away,
and he resolved to learn enough nearly overnight,
      to convince the Nazis that his life held any value at all.

Bargain

Please don't think I am trying to slide out of our deal,
for I am no weasel.
It's just that, after nearly 60 years of attempted compliance,
I might better appreciate to what terms we actually agreed.

Perhaps it would be easier to call our deal a "bargain,"
instead of frightfully formal title, "The Covenant,"
but considering the continued inheritance now by 200 generations,
I concede that it is more than just another business negotiation.

Still, it sounds pretty bizarre on the surface:
You let me live for a while and call myself one of the "chosen
people,"
and in exchange, someone slices off a ring of skin
from around my sexual organ.

You promise us a share in a piece of real estate
that is two-thirds desert,
surrounded by countless others, who have made this same deal,
each subgroup citing a further promise of commitment.

Please don't think that I am complaining,
for I know my place,
understand that the alternative is fiery death or subtle assimilation,
accept that other people do good deeds and receive praise.

Also, I understand that you cannot be fooled,
as you are omniscient and omnipotent and all that,
so I won't try any weak explanations, like,
"I'm experimenting with pork."

Incidentally, it might have been nice to know the taste of pork, or
what it feels like to fiddle with a foreskin,
but I do understand consequences, that upon the walls of Jericho,
both my deceit and my descent would have been cut off.

So I have come to realize that we were not chosen to suffer
any more or less that anyone else,
but rather to carry a memory trace,
a responsibility threading through human time,

of the difference between cleanliness and defilement,
light and darkness, progress and degradation,
upcast in the face of society, impossible to ignore.
So I will keep our bargain, and circumcise my son.

August Sestina

Numbered days of summer grow late,
now enter the month of August.
Sun so hot it could melt a glacier,
northern flora surpass anticipation,
defy the zodiac Virgin,
and submit to events they do not dread.

For it is only Humans who dread
that they will learn too late,
compare wilderness to a virgin,
and label sullied spirits as august,
disguise frailty with the anticipation
of salvation, before the next glacier.

But our lake was formed by a dam, not a glacier,
and at first, it is only sizzling asphalt that I dread,
bathing suit beneath my pants in anticipation,
on a hot back-seat denying that again we will be late
for a frolic across the beaches of August,
while Dr. Dad counsels a patient to remain a virgin,

or administers medicines to an ex-virgin,
as Mom does her errand at the pace of a glacier,
doing their best to waste another day of August,
and I watch the waning sun and dread,
at best, one cold dip, then picnic so late,
that the setting sun devours anticipation.

Years later, the night sky will *define* anticipation,
as I imagine unveilings of my own tender virgin,
to which stage, like beach trips, I arrived late,
learning how any son can melt a glacier
if he does not immerse himself in dread,
but rather, in the joyous growth of August.

For the blueberry bears its fruit in August,
then drops dry seed in anticipation
of coming winter, never withering in dread,
but seeks a patch of soil virgin,
moistened by water from melting glacier,
a bed nature makes to emulate.

Sun of August, shrinking glacier,
anticipation encounters dread,
dreams of virgins, never late.

From Whence I Came*

I.

When the loose knee cartilage suddenly locked,
as he scrambled blindly through dense brambles,
frantically racing away from the soggy bank of the Prut,
muck still encrusting his hands and wrists,
flying in chunks from his bare feet and ankles,
he flew helplessly into a young alder,
burning his shoulder against its smooth bark,
anointing his torso with welts and punctures,
yet he screamed only in silence.

Jacob was a large man, and it took a dark night
to cover his muffled swim across the border,
in one immense burst of controlled courage,
not comparable to the charade of innocence,
that brought him 100 miles from Rezeni,*
south along the Dnestr River,
then west through fertile farmlands of Moldavia,
to pass between the Czar's border patrols,
until that moment when he slipped into the murky waters,
risking his life to forge otter-style toward freedom.

Although he did not look much like a Jew,
with red hair to almost match his bleeding skin,
Jacob could not blend into the local populace
while still naked, scratched and hobbling,
so he stole some rags and food scraps,
hid and slept during the day,
and made his way through northern Romania,
along night-veiled wagon roads,
ever practicing his new name,
Shiovitz, the son of Shia,
an untraceable Russian label,
that would not endanger his father,
Yishia, Hebrew for Isaiah,
or any of the other Zborofsky family,
scattered throughout the Ukraine.

Unlike his biblical namesake,
Jacob accepted the role of second son,

never begrudging his older brother an army exemption,
but hell if he would serve the Czar in Siberian winter,
so he visited the Jewish graveyard one last time,
kissed his elderly father on a stubbly cheek,
hugged his sobbing brother and sister,
and set off for Romania.

Hunger played tricks upon Jacob's mind,
as he lay in a cold ditch outside Hirlau,
a small village 200 miles north of Bucharest,
for he clearly heard his sister laughing,
his brother telling jokes in Yiddish,
and his father chastising their irreverence.
"A Shonda," scolded the ancient voice,
"Have you no respect?"
The laughing eyes turned to terror,
As Jacob's hulking and tattered body,
filled the doorway of the Bernstein cottage,
where diminutive Devorah quickly brought soup,
washed his wounds,
gathered garments from her step-brothers,
and soon became the bride of Jacob Shiovitz.
"Size is of no consequence," Jacob told her,
"Your heart is the biggest I have ever known."

Jacob found happiness in Romania with Devorah
who affectionately called him "Yankel,"
but peace and freedom were more elusive.
Borders changed and Cossacks burned Hirlau to the ground,
swatted Devorah's step-sister and father like flies
as she watched from the same ditch where Jacob had lain,
clutching baby Max to her breast, to stifle his sounds,
praying they would not see her other children among the cabbages,
her Yankel behind the woodpile,
vowing that one day they would all leave this evil land behind.

II.

Max stood near the bow of the steamship,
wind numbing his unshaven face,
wondered what Calgary, Alberta would promise,
how long it would take for him and sister Rose
to earn the passage for his parents, brother and three other sisters,

but warmed as he thought, "At least this time,
a Shiovitz is crossing the water like a man."

III.

The shop in Detroit was piled high with store fixtures,
so that Louie had only one corner of a bench,
where the mechanical guts of a cash register,
were organized in the order he dismantled them.
Fortunately, Louie had a knack for repairing machines,
even enjoyed the long hours of cleaning and reassembly,
for his father Max could be a tough son-of-a-gun with slackers,
perhaps because two of Louie's eleven brothers and sisters
had died during that trucking business attempt up in Bad Axe,
from Infant Diarrhea and Pneumonia, people said,
but Max was never sure,
and he would crack heads, if need be, to keep his family alive.
His wife, Bella, was much taller and stronger than Devorah,
but raising twelve children through difficult times
had begun to sap Bella's strength, so it seemed natural
that Louie's older brothers and sisters took on parental duties,
and he soon learned that if he wanted anything extra,
he would have to earn it himself.

When Dr. Louis Shiovitz graduated from medical school,
he could reflect on the creative diligence that delivered tuition,
such as typing up and selling lecture notes to his classmates,
or taking jobs he could handle with his face in an anatomy text.
When he married Belleen, daughter of a scrap metal dealer,
he thought Sam and Minnie Reichstein to be somewhat well off,
but not the reason two of Belleen's brothers
later shortened their last name to "Rich."

Louis never questioned the importance of fighting for freedom,
and near the end of World War II, on his airbase hospital
in Washington D.C., Belleen gave birth
to the second of her four children, all boys,
to this poet, who has not once risked his life for freedom,
who is left to wonder, along with 40 first cousins
and hundreds who share the legacy of the name,
what one man must have endured,
in his passage from nowhere to nowhere,
keeping his religion,

but sacrificing his secular identity
to the more important name
of Freedom.

Unholy Herring

The old man stuck a fork into the silken mass of sour cream,
pulled out a writhing hunk of onion-wrapped herring,
and slipped it between his waiting lips,
ignoring drips of excess whiteness that bedecked his gray beard.
Instead he reveled in the instantaneous pleasure,
the momentary distraction that affirms continuity,
in a life beset by constant struggle.

Staring at the foreign newspaper next to his plate,
his weary eyes tried to merge two matching headlines,
of grisly bombings in Jerusalem and Baghdad,
and twin pictures beneath the heavy black words,
that showed legs protruding from rubble and wreckage,
blown from one picture into the other.

"This should punch a hole in their red herring."
the old man fumed, his eyes almost closed in anger,
"Even the biggest apologists cannot explain this one away!"
Tears appeared at the corner of the old man's eyes,
as he read about slain United Nations peace workers,
mangled children and innocent bystanders.
He sucked down another slimy morsel,
with eyes now completely shut in isolation.

"They speak in the name of the people," he said aloud,
"but the people are too ignorant or too afraid to resist."
Staunching the aftertaste, he bit into a slice of black rye,
then reset his pallet by drinking deeply of plain water.
"A man must live by his principles," he whispered.
"No matter who says it, when I hear it,
I know the difference between right and wrong."

The old man took the napkin from his undershirt,
wiped his beard, then thoroughly washed his face,
broke the wrap on a crisply starched shirt,
and reached into the closet for his formal suit,
bearing sash and seal of the Norwegian Embassy,
in preparation to face one more day without permission
to publicly express an opinion.

Buying Time

"Always make rock solid investments,"
said Father at my adulthood,
"Plan for the long term.
Short trends can't be trusted."
He spoke again, and I listened intently.
"Don't put your eggs in one basket,"
he warned, "Diversify, diversify."

Armed with this advice,
after years without excess,
the moment arrived to test a small sum.
"Solid as Concrete," boasted the swampland brochure,
"Foundation of America," rambled the railroad report,
"Gateway to the Future," read the Tech public offering,
yet I demurred, for every stock had its risk,
it seemed impossible to safely plan for the future,
as I continued to age, to run out of time.

"Aha," the eureka moment exploded,
"In time.….I shall invest, and just in time.
For time will endure as no solid substance,
but more so, will always be there for the taking,
and diverse, why the combinations are endless.
What could be better that the buying of time?"

But the purchase potential was still filled with pitfalls,
as when the executive could give me just a minute,
or the doctor offered one hour and replaced it with another,
and the airlines lost an entire night of my vacation,
in fact, it appeared hopeless until I discovered
a solitary non-solicitous soul.

"How long will you love me?" as a wise shopper I asked.
"Every second, every minute of eternity," she answered.
"No more risk than the swampland," I appraised,
then replied while the offer still pended,
"Sure, I'll buy that!"

Pot-Bound

The plant topples, cracks its terra cotta base,
sends pebbles bouncing along the brick path,
crumples branches and leaves,
reveals drain tiles hanging on exposed roots.
This product of seventeen years of our nurturing love
lies momentarily upended.

When just a seedling, sprouted in a tiny peat pot,
we nudged strands of moss away from the stem,
to prevent damping off by unseen fungal forces,
above a precisely mixed potting soil,
watched so that excess water did not rot the roots,
let it dry between drinks, and kept it nearly pot-bound.

Those early years were a period of challenge,
with exposure to every healthy environment,
ceaseless feedings and changes of pottery,
messy seepages, as strands undertook their trims,
and ever so slowly, the plant increased in strength,
learning to resist the whims of nature.

Later growth occurred in spurts of gangly appendages,
followed by appearance of the first shy flower,
but who could keep pace with the constant need,
logical arguments to purchase ever larger pots,
endless cries for more space,
pleas to escape confinement of the house?

So in compromise, the plant was placed outside,
to experience the unfiltered song of the sun,
the stimulating touch of wild summer breezes,
that excited leaves and branches,
and caused roots to expand so uncontrollably
that it finally burst free to seek a place of its own.

Along the Oregon Coast

There is a seagull that is always present
in the parking-lot overlook for Cape Perpetua,
or at least it was there both times
when I toured this
puzzling turnout.

Yet the spectacular vision below
was neither a Cape nor Perpetual,
but an inlet,
clearly formed in recent geologic time
by a fault line through solid rock,
which has been exploited by crashing waves,
battered into a broad expanse at the mouth,
and only a few inches wide where it moves inland,
except for an open tub-like chamber,
that explodes with foam and spray
a few seconds after each wave disappears
into the slit at the base of the rocks.

In truth this inlet is no more perpetual
than that seagull in the lot above,
but named by ego-centered folly,
and paced with the faster clock,
that measures nature in Human time.

So it is with another sight, just an hour to the north,
where below the light at Yachina Head,
an abandoned basalt quarry
has been developed for a tide pool tour,
and at low tide, even wheel chairs
can move between the man-raised pools,
permitting ease for view and touch
of teeming lives that occupy
this zone of violent change,
or at least man tried it for a few short years,
before the ocean changed its mind
and bestowed upon the paths and pools,
a three-foot depth of choking sand.

Yaquina Head Light

The black, wrought-iron staircase
circles upward
one hundred ten steps,
with landings for only
three brief pauses,
before a climber can achieve the light.

An outside shell of concrete blocks
protects the steely spine
from ever-present winds
and wintry gales,
from splash and spray above the cliff,
that have long since eroded
the Keeper's cabin,
rotted
the animal shelters and outbuildings,
to leave only the adjoining
concrete cottage.

At the very top, an amazing dome
of parallel prisms and lenses
directs the light
of tiny bulbs, once flames,
into parallel beams,
powerful enough to be visible
twenty miles out to sea.

It began over a century ago
with shovels,
as men dug deeply into rock,
laid a foundation that would support
a beacon
to guide home the wanderer.

For those engulfed in a shroud of fog,
drifting
far off-shore,
where spirits dissolve
for lack of hope,
any blessed glimpse of land,

engenders
strength forgotten.

Yet of all those rescued souls,
none likely placed a single block
upon the concrete edifice,
or tended the lard-burning flame,
but were left ashore,
seeking a way to repay their debt
toward that eternal struggle
between life and disarray.

Eighteen Fence Posts

The wire-cable fence above Nye Beach
marks the deepest penetration
of human design upon nature,
for on one side, a concrete deck
supports picnic tables and a ramp,
on the other, a wide expanse
of pebble-speckled sand
glistens from the receding tide
that turns crashing waves
into predators,
who creep forty feet landward,
before they disappear exhausted
beneath the beach.

The cable fence is strung
through man-sized wooden posts,
spaced precisely,
as if two people stretched arms
to bear between them
a picnic basket or duffle bag.

Seventeen of these posts
directly face the sea;
an eighteenth
falls back just a little,
but fronts three more posts
that project inland
toward the concrete ramp.

And on each of the eighteen frontier posts,
facing into the ceaseless wind,
a white-headed Herring Gull
is perched,
bestowing a crown
upon the guano-robed pickets,
that divide man's development
from the untamed fury.

On frequent occasions, an excess gull
swoops down,

engages a resident post-sitter
and takes his place
as a sea-gazing sentinel,
freeing the displaced bird
to challenge
yet another sitting gull.

But no hovering gull
ever settles
upon one of the three inland posts,
for gull-perching
is anything but random.

I have seen gulls standing on rows of rooftops,
perched singly
or in groups of twos and threes,
spaced
with some knowable regularity,
seen them massed
above a fisherman's wharf,
strung across the eaves
every eighteen inches
like gray pearls,

and I have watched the discipline erode
among a multitude
swarming
just above the scaling sinks,
where one can
begin to realize
the frenzied connection
between civilized behavior
        and the brutality
                of survival.

Oh Tree

"Oh tree, oh tree, open up for me…"
he thought, and his gray cap glowed green,
as he landed in the branches of a lurching larch,
opened the hatch and hastened to the turf.

"Sweet, sweet, sweet, I'll kiss-iss-iss you…"
he suddenly heard, and cocked his head skyward,
as a yellow warbler broadcast from a distant branch.
"A bird… in a tree. How absurd."

"Oh eyes, oh eyes, refocus for me…"
he thought, and his goggles glowed gray
as he watched the feathered machine
attempt to balance on the branch with its wheels.

"Sweet, sweet, sweet, I'll…"
"Smash to the turf, you reprogrammed misfit,"
he uttered without understanding,
toward the shattered raft of gears and feathers.

"I guess I should pick up the pieces,"
he thought, as his shoes glowed silver,
little wheels appeared beneath his soles,
and he skated over to retrieve the broken bird.

"Oh plane, oh plane, its time to go home…"
he thought, while his cap glowed yellow,
and as his aircraft alit from its perch,
it slowly retracted its claws.

French Markets

The Parisian fruit vendor on Rue Cler tolerates no cherry picking,
but takes your bag and randomly shovels in the ruby morsels.
His open display pleases the passerby with a patchwork
of ripening yellows and rouge.

Fringing the cobblestone street, other stands arouse your senses.
The smell of Epoisse whispers of salivation
from beside wheels of white Brie and blocks of orange,
while a ceramic dish of sample cheeses cannot be ignored.

The aroma of freshly baked breads begs for attention,
and shoppers stand in line before a stall,
then emerge with a stiff baguette or plump country loaf,
or caress the morning with a chocolate croissant.

This flakey delight floats a memory of the road to Dijon,
where a heavenly patisserie perfected the petit-dejeuner:
beneath the detailed sketch of a horse, created in chocolate,
café au lait, with a tiny sweet egg nested in your spoon,

and of snacking outside the Cathedral at Chartes,
upon treasures of the weekly Farmers Market,
where white asparagus was stacked in mounds,
and fishwives sliced loaves of a mysterious jellied redness,

and of the Parisian café below the market on Montmarte.
Above, it had been too frantic to sit and eat,
but was perfect for watching others sit for a portrait,
or purchase mementoes among the mass of competing artisans.

It is quieter along the Seine.
Here the stalls are spread apart,
and used booksellers quietly converse,
in synchrony with the lapping waves.

Magnolia

In April,
the whole tree is a flower
awaiting leaves,
tight buds of fleshy lobes
cast outside in magenta,
fringes fading to white,
then half open,
become pink-glazed teacups
complete with sepal saucers,
and opened full,
radiate six snowy petals
around a bristly button,
finally to grace the ground
with a royal carpet.

Scud

There is no end to it,
this surety that today's worry
will be the last of them,
that tomorrow will bring sweet peace
without pain,
or maybe it will be the day after,
when a solution will firm from shadows,
and expectation rise to proclaim,
"Life is good,"
with such exuberance
that I will stand up from my desk,
tucked by the knee-wall beneath a low ceiling,
and once again knock my head.

Prophet Loss Statements*

Two prophets, Elijah and Miriam, fold tallisim in Heaven's laundry
to provide meaningful gifts for B'nai Mitzvah morning,
most of which were returned to Heaven after burial, barely used.

The two prophets had worked together since the 1980s,
when modern zealots immersed Miriam into Elijah's song, *Eliahu
HaNavi*,
and implored worshipers to sip with their wine, some water.

Miriam became meshed with m*a-yim*, water,
because she tracked the basket of Moses in the Nile,
and pranced laughing with timbrels by the Sea of Reeds.

Elijah and wine were wedded from at least the Middle Ages,
as Jews opened their doors for him at the *seder*,
to show neighbors they imbibed no blood, only fruit of the vine.

In life, both prophets had earned a measure of respect:
Miriam nagged at Moses for marrying that Cushite woman,
but balanced her scales with a talent for finding water.

Elijah's talent was to portend or predict great events,
until he passed the mantle to Elisha, who seemed to exceed his
teacher,
breathed life back into a boy that died.

Now, to make a little repentance for the High Holidays,
Elijah finally admits to Miriam that really he was a bit of a lush,
which loosed those visions, and led him to invent artificial respiration.

Miriam responds that it was stressful to be the big sister of Moses,
he rarely listened to her, so she did what she liked,
and always she wanted to dance, to celebrate water, wine, whatever.

Both agree it was a stretch to label them as seers,
but to convince folks otherwise, Heaven knows,
no reason had been foreseen.

Hedges

Fences have edges, but hedges are graded,
hedges grow full, while fences are gaunt,
fences are simple in parallel and lattice,
hedges are weavings of leaves and of branches.

When new, fences shine from coats of fresh paint,
when old, they gray and gradually rot,
hedges start sparse, then grow thick from the ground,
a waxy green wall, a more gentle surround.

Wedgwood Rock

A thousand faces of black and gray basalt coat the behemoth,
whose peak looms high over loam-covered sands,
halfway up the glacial ridge that holds this giant rock,
one such face viewing the Ravenna valley,
another scans snow capped peaks of the Olympic Mountains
and a third casts toward the Cascade Range but is screened by the ridge,
as those that once looked to Capitol Hill or regarded Mount Rainier,
now are hampered by houses and trees inside the plat
whose name reflects this room-sized lump of frozen lava,
that was pushed like a pebble by walls of ice a mile high,
to sit exposed aside the ridge and convince every thoughtful observer
that it is significant in ways that can be seen in its faces,
like the one that bore witness to vows of peace
among local Native American tribes,
while another observed a pact with Army envoys,
like its low faces speak to children on bicycles,
or to dogs that piddle and poop in canid respect,
and although The City long ago declared climbing activity illegal,
experienced technicians still finger interfacial ridges,
and novices grab the rope hanging from one of the six trees
that hide "Big Rock" from drivers of automobiles
who speed past without the slightest thought upon its effects,
such as I wonder if it were only chance
when first I beheld it,
that I could not help but reach out to touch a face,
my face,
and a few days later found our home and future,
        four houses south of Wedgwood Rock.

Cathy Shiovitz
Photo by Tom Hefferan

Author as Alzheimer's afflicted Marvin Price in the SJTC production of The Last Seder, by Jennifer Maisel in 2011. From left: Author, Carolyn "Puddin" Cox, Floyd Reichman, Carol Silverstein, Barbara Goldhammer, Jo Merrick, Dawn Cornell Townes, Al Hillel, Jeff Novack, Navarre Moore, and Susan King.

"The Three Rabbis" roast the guest speaker at Camp Kesher on Vashon Island, WA. From left, author, Maurice Varon, Gino Gianola.

4

SURVIVE AND PREVAIL

2008 - 2015

Little Si

High up the side of Little Si,
in filtered light through firs that hide its size,
rises a face of sheer rock,
the direct route to the summit.
There climbers cling to ledges and clefts,
slowly slip ropes into clips
that glow gold in the morning sun.
Blocks of basalt, some large as buses,
are scattered about the cool base of the wall.
Upon them lichens and mosses
mark the rate of nature's change.
For less hardy hikers,
a rustic trail snakes toward the top.
Suddenly, a painted bench
with a tarnished plaque
for someone lost on Everest.
No one sits on the bench.
Decaying logs suffice for the living.

Abraham Reflects

Because I rejected the idea of gods in stone idols,
we parted from the ignorant proto-Persians,
wandered in worn sandals on warm dunes,
and plodded toward the land of promise.

As howling winds swept the wastelands,
stung our eyes, rang in our ears,
is it a wonder I witnessed divine presence,
heard the voice in my head?

One single Godly insight in a life so full of blindness:
I sold honor for survival telling the king of Gerar
that wife Sarah was my sister,
cast my first son out of camp to quell a lover's quarrel,
nearly burned the second boy upon a hilltop altar.

Truly my dad, Terah, only called me Son.
To the children of my children
I was the source of many nations,
Very Lofty Father,
Av-raham.

Yet I destroyed for my growing boys
that bond of love between normal brothers,
and their offspring still invoke my God,
even as they kill each other.

Sadly, child psychology could not be found
in my sack of tools;
it would have to be founded
            by someone else's father.

Waves

From an airplane above the Hawaiian Pacific,
I view the sunny sea as weaves of waves,
some are expanses of blinding white,
others deep navy,
studded with diamonds.

Leaving shore, I had noticed aquamarine shallows
morphed into patches of whitecaps
that foamed suddenly to life
slowly dissolved
seemed to express
some personal distance between themselves,
perhaps a reflection of dramatic
collisions
between waves that behave more politely
far away from land.

Now over the open ocean I see waves that move
in exactly the same direction,
each stretching widely
to disappear from focus
in an endless series of swells.

I search the heaving waters for a different direction
another caliber of thread,
am instantly rewarded
by a series of parallel scratches
nearly perpendicular to the first and much smaller.

After I find five separate wave sets
in five distinct directions,
I am satisfied.

The driver of the tour bus down Mauna Kea
had shown us where the wild burros thrive,
now when everyone else was asleep,
he shared with me his love for surfing,
his excitement at hearing of distant storms.

He told how winds make waves
of many directions and sizes,
and as they travel toward the open sea,
how smaller waves become swallowed up, merged,
form regular swells that cross the ocean
until they hit a shallow
rise up to break upon themselves.
Some, like the famous "Pipeline," are enormous.

He learned to wait with board attached by ankle cuff,
ready to climb up at just the right moment
with arms and knees bent
to slice under a foaming fold
slide parallel to shore in one direction
then suddenly reverse course,
riding a wave toward the beach,
to dismount at the last moment
paddle back
to where the wild burros gather.

Safe Harbor for Starlings

They don't like to hang alone
these star-studded squabblers
these black-feathered racketeers
who gather on the silo catwalks of Cargil's pier
to peck-up kernels escaped from hulls of vessels,
replacing grain with splattered guano.

I tried to disperse them with recorded alarm calls.

They quickly ignored my feeble efforts,
rained white over my career as a behavioral consultant,
displayed their generations of honing that gangster trick
of artful contempt.

Falling Leaf

A
leaf
releases its twig-hold
falls spinning around its spine
indirectly to the ground
where heaps of fanlet kin
softly weave the new arrival
into the top-skin of a feathery pile
bright yellow and waxy
that melts from below
translucent nets of veins
then into flakes
that worm-fed
form the loam
of yesterday's
pride....and
tomorrow's
rebirth.

Exemptions

In February a small sack of silk
fits tight against a window frame,
warmly wraps tiny spiders.

Glaciers of May melted to icy streams
flood valleys, erode loam,
spare a sapling atop moist stones.

The August sun grills a lawn to wool,
leaves one patch of green
still cool in a pattern shadow.

In November the ginkgo bares its branches
as straw fans spiral to earth…
on the maple, a shriveled fist hangs fast.

Lost in June

Walk the new-grown fields of June,
rural edges of warm moist air
alive with buzz and humm, chirp and trill,
with sweet song and soulful chant,
rye grasses high up the juniper
goldenrod thick with anticipation.

Watch a sunlit hawk soar
above separated stands of trees
as sparrows dart between them,
goldfinches skim the meadows,
tits flit in bushes
and a wood thrush
rustles through leafy litter.

Peering inside a small cedar
you flush a robin to a nearby alder,
in the shadows - a mud strewn nest
with three naked nestlings,
fragile, beaks agape,
begging for enough to survive
the short June night.

Transformation

The man with a stooped torso
who scooped tossed salad slowly onto a plate
neither cursed the pain from gnarly fingers
nor was pleased with the selection of toppings.

He shuffled toward a table
girded for social contact,
the closest mimic of family comfort
where mention of a name could elicit a smile.

Now the trophies were stowed in cartons,
silver safely shipped to Donna's condo
and the tattered address book,
just pages of a crossed out past.

At the table one man looked up,
coughed, cleared his throat
engaged him in quiet conversation:
Sure, it was a pity the Tigers lost again…
Sorry that he was not up for a game of cards…
Yes, the best in the business is Dr. Bennett…

Green Movements

Slow, slow, slow…
the only rush

is the reed in his yard
beneath the hush of a weeping willow,

or the trickle of rain off a sod-laden roof
to a bog in the lawn that he dug,

or the song of a wren through waterfall mist
moved by the hand of the sun,

or a breeze in the props of a tireless mill
and the chant of our earth sharing heat.

His world is a tribute to nature's embrace
to remind of the peace we forget.

De Mean Peoples

De mean peoples, dey gots dose demon eyes.
Dey gots to dash dem brains. Dey gots to demon-ize.

Dem nasty minds, why dey gots to be so mean?
Why dey gots to ruin dem reps, dem lives dey gots to ream?

Always dey demeaning, never aks de meaning,
Never hear de crying, never care de dying.

De meanies say dey meaning well,
Dey ask yo mama's health, (dey cackles when she fells.)

Dem meany peoples gots to hurts
Cries out for comfort words

For dems I gots no time to pray...
I just gets out de way.

Symbols

As the Rabbi told of three strangers
foreshadowing God's plan
to destroy two cities
if Abraham could not produce
one righteous man,
I saw out the window
a murder of crows,
group of 13 evenly spaced birds,
swoop downward
over the community garden,
when suddenly in mid-air
the lead bird was pecked
in the head by a follower.

That night,
when I awoke
with left arm pain
after moving a cement birdbath
to over-winter in the shed,
I flew out of bed
downed three crushed aspirin,
assured myself it was
a purely symbolic gesture.

Air at the Fair

The air at the Fair braces your face
with the promise of frost,
carries shrieks from ecstatic kids,
snorts from enormous swine,
banter of carnival pitchmen and bantam hens,
scents of sheep, soiled hay
and five kinds of pie.

The air at the Fair is always unfair,
wraps your mind in a veil of haze,
leads you to eat corn dogs, cotton candy,
stand in an hour long line for a scone
then take a bone-jarring ride
on a stomach inverter,
squeeze between posts, climb up railings,
toss coins across slippery platters,
wear a pickle pin, win bamboo canes,
surrender to the merits of a slicer-dicer,
drive fully exhausted down the long road home.

Like Eagles Soar*

From the mansion
green lawn stretched unbroken to the salty strait, save for a solitary
tree
tall enough to shade the couple taking vows,
a newly ordained officiant,
ring-bearing best man and bridesmaid, wearing near-formality
modified
for slow
paced
island
life
and the couple's love for all things natural.

Leading the party down the aisle
Kabuki dancers in white-face
demanded a pause
in decorum
as they entertained through a transition from strict tradition
to   free   expression
formal robes
          thrown
to   the   wind.

As the rings passed from bearers to fingers of bride and groom
                     two   eagles
                          from
West   and   East
soared above and crossed paths
before the eyes of astonished beholders,
a blessing
to this and every couple who understand
the holiness
of the   wild.

Beneath the Surface Still

Waves splash over my legs
on the ledge where I pull on flippers
adjust mask and snorkel
amid the sounds of swimmers and mynahs
foaming surf, sea gulls, gusts of wind.

I pitch forward with fear
of shocking cold
of a mouthful of ocean,
but the water is warm
mask tightly sealed,
loud breaths of air,
loud breaths of air,
loud breaths of air,
everything else is completely
still.

I look down at another world
where a dozen yellow tangs,
hand-sized with finger-mouths,
swarm over one spot on the coral,
nipping with tiny lips.

The coral itself
in reds, browns, yellows
in mounds, pillars, fans, candelabras
is razor sharp
and shields black urchins
with long poisonous
spines.

Time floats by
with colorful butterfly fish,
reddish wrasses, long narrow needlefish,
pufferfish, parrotfish, moray eels,
even a grazing sea turtle,
until my throat feels dry
legs tire,
time to turn back toward the ledge.

I round the corner of a large coral bed
three firm flipper kicks from shore,
do not notice the lower tide,
waves that strike rocks to my side,
break over the snorkel tube
filling my mouth
with seawater.

To blow water
back up the tube,
for an instant
I must
stop swimming,
tread water,
ignore
the next large wave that knocks me sideways
into the barely submerged coral.
I feel a burn,
kick violently three times toward the ledge,
haul out
bleeding at the knee.

An old Hawaiian man says
I should rub it with a leaf
of the *ah-**low**-eiy*.
Somehow I understand he means the fleshy aloe
growing in a large clump
nearby where a mongoose had darted.

It stops the bleeding.
I look at my knee.
It has been tattooed with honeycombs,
at the center of each hexagon
a tiny circle,
a souvenir of Hawaii.

It Matters

It all matters.
The drops of rain that run
behind your gutter,
the drops that find
the pot on your porch.

It matters
how you nudged the overhang
where you placed the pot
when you planted the flower.

Even that second of uncertainty
before you yield to a billow of pleasure
that brings your child to life,
matters.

The rotten
fascia board
finally fixed,
the toddler
pauses below
picks
a geranium bloom
and laughs.

Dead Gnat on my Shower Curtain

He was a gnat.
He died a gnatural death.

from the equator

the equator and politics are all about spin
                       all
                          about
                             spin
all about the direction we travel
to where we think we travel
want to travel
where someone wants us to arrive

the equator is the longest distance around the earth
around   the   earth
                in the direction we move
politics is maddening
always goes the longest way
no shortcuts
for every attempt
repercussions

The earth never spins backwards
                         never
                   spins
           backwards
no matter how we wish

but sometimes after
many many millennia
magnetic poles switch
         pole
      switches
         pole

Wholeness Returned

A fallen oak has left a hole in the forest canopy,
centered
on giant roots that twisted aside tannic soil
to leave a shallow pit.

From there the massive trunk made a radius of destruction,
everything directly beneath
flattened,
a saber slash in the flank of encroaching neighbors.

When it tumbled on itself
cracked branches sliced
surrounding vegetation like giant scythes,
leaving evidence of former glory
    engraved   in the woods,
and a larger circle in which competition
        was shaded out.

The passage was swift,
some creaks and groans, sharp snaps, an extended crash,
haunting echoes
   haunting echoes
then complete
quiet.

Every bird fell silent.

Dust rose to fill the gap in the canopy.

Now the air begins to clear.
The reedy song of a thrush
sneaks through distant trees.
Squirrels churr, shake branches.
Worms, millipedes stir the dust-topped litter.
Sun floods the hole with healing warmth.

An untouched seedling
pale and weak
moves its only leaf
to face the light.

Overjoyed*

The dead must be overjoyed
to find that heaven is exactly as advertised:
a steady 72 degrees Fahrenheit,
sunny,
faint breeze with a scent of salt water,
no dyspepsia, jealousy or crime.

Predictably, the newly dead
race through heaven
on wings and legs that will never tire,
test hand-springs and air loops,
crash into each other and laugh,
pull others' halos down over their shoulders
to try and pin arms and wings.

As this happened every day for eons
the long-term angels are not amused
but float past in fixation
on some window of ethereal vision,
until distracted by a now bored newcomer
who asks what they are watching.

Still capable of bemused smirks
the ancient angels explain
how they tired of watching worlds
of bizarre acts and malfunctions
or the interplay of good versus evil,
had heard every lofty thought,
were benumbed by every human behavior.

The newly dead knit incorporeal brows,
wonder if heaven is a hell of boredom ...
and then they begin to watch
and learn
of eternity and possibility
  always possibility.

Silent Travelers in a Bubble Chamber*

Little bubbles
shoulder to shoulder
show me the path of a particle
too small for a microscope to resolve.

Since
    before ears
particles have lived in silence,
    before eyes
they have traced lonely roads.

Today
they cannot know they are noticed
but may
interact with me from a distance.

Shy girls
who walk across the street
from boys,
look straight ahead...

yet catch a glance,
or somehow feel
eyes watching them,
put an extra bounce in each step
a little rhythm
while they fight to keep
a flush down from the cheek
stop a stiffening neck
from giving them away.

Gathering

Bodies are together for a sort of picnic
where it is cloudy all morning and it looks like rain
and maybe the hot, humid air
will hold until you are ready to leave
or big black clouds will not suddenly blot out the sun
before the deluge drenches you to the skin...
except really it is no picnic
but more like a reunion of cousins
and everyone hugs everyone else,
you tell them how important they are to you
then go back to not calling for another decade
while knowing that as a group
you depend upon them like brothers
who will bail you out when you are down
after countless times
when mother was out shopping
they had wrestled you to the ground...
except it really is no reunion
but more like shopping at a grocery store
where you have a large cart
that moves down a long narrow aisle
and it holds boxes of cereal and ice cream
but also eggs and lettuce
fragile groceries and firmer ones
that together get along civilly
as long as you move fast
get home before they melt together into a glob
and you don't know exactly from what tree
the cereal box was made or where the oats were grown
and don't really care how the oat got its minerals
even though they were sucked from dirt
and some of that dirt came from cow dung
and parts of dirt came from space
raining down as dust that survived such heat
that maybe it glowed red in the night sky.
Yes, a gathering like that...
except instead of cereal
it is your heart
and the ice cream is a fist
and they get along with your eyes and ears

long enough for you to run down the aisle
and get home before the heavens burst.

That May

The buds that may unfurl a leaf
stem from the stems of summer.

The blooms of May that so enthrall
are fruit of the fruits of August.

Tender greens that paint spring trees
spring from the spring of September.

Wafting scents that so benumb
are wrought from the rot of November.

Treetop chorales that captivate
muster from the bluster of March.

It cannot return unless reversed
this prime performance unrehearsed.

Winged Warriors*

Above a pond
a dragonfly darts
alights on a swaying stalk,
gossamer wings barely visible above
his drab body.

Suddenly a rival intrudes
unbending
past that reedy border post
where the dragonfly at rest
takes flight
with abdomen abducted
to fully display
a white warning-patch
and boldly chases the brassy intruder
back across the pond,

until he blunders
past a prominent cat-tail rush,
his rival's frontier,
as extensor muscles retract in fear.

Twin pairs of wings now bank and beat
across the pond in full retreat.

Third Generation

The First Generation knew wheat
how to run a John Deere
The song of the thrush
and made out in the meadow.

The Second Generation knew the law
how to habeas a corpus
the song of the jail bird
and made out in the stock market.

The Third Generation knew the moon
how to run a spaceship
the song of the thruster
and made it out of the solar system.

Meteor

He entered earth's atmosphere covered in dependence and hope
already the product of growth at such an incredible rate
that he immediately started to brightly glow
so people took notice and would remark
what a promising future lay ahead,
but they did not comment on
the small flaming pieces
spewing from his soul   as
he raced through
in rapid descent
to finally land
in the earth,
a burnt out
remnant   of
promise
and of
deed.

Marco Polo Returns

When Marco returned
the city was larger.
People noticed his spices
that improved their meals.

Soon tired of stories
on alien culture,
they queried instead
on weapons and trade.

As soon as he could
Marco wrote it all down,
got dressed before dawn
and slipped out of town.

Kitten Whiskers

Before she opens her eyes
I gently stroke her whiskers
ask if she knows who I am.
Her muted answer,
"Feed me."

Kitten whiskers skim the spaces around their faces
to protect unsteady heads,
legs wrestling paws on a polished floor.

Each whisker probes the darkness
to illumine a wall, pair of shoes,
ball of something soft… that…slightly… moves.

Each stalk tutors these stalkers
of window shade chords and sunbeams,
whenever tiny teeth miss their target.

Each whisker is an artisan's tool,
curved by a clawed paw, carefully honed
on the rough surface of a loving tongue.

Sled Husky

Take heart amid
your weariness
harnessed like a sled husky
through endless
mushes for snovival,
still turned to nurture
inherent potential.

The promise of your generation
scurries beneath the snow
not gauged in depth of powder
over strange terrain
but measured in ideas,
the global melt water
of coming spring.

Omen

A cat dropped from a tree
before my feet,
shrieked, claws extended,
bolted behind a fence.

Then a crow swooped
clawed my hat,
twice.

Later a black ball
bounced down the asphalt,
ran up the driveway
hit me in the ankles,
stopped at the base of a black locust.

I remember I stepped over
a little sinkhole today,
saw another one open
deep and black
as I rounded a corner.

Are these odder events than
water rising to the top of a Redwood?
shoots emerging from soil after the winter?
a fledgling flapping aloft?

Today I watched a single blowfly
flow silent through the room,
disappear.

The Butcher's Apprentice

The butcher takes lives to give life.
He is part of a cycle,
like water, carbon or Schwinn.
Before work he sips his coffee black.
He cannot be drowsy when the cleaver falls.
Fluids and giblets are flushed from sight.

I am the butcher's apprentice.
My coffee is decaf, and I cannot kill a calf.
Instead, I brush fluids and giblets from sight
broom them into an opening in the floor
eat them later as sausage.

The butcher kills and I clean.
There is no money in sweeping guts.
No money, but lots of smells, gaggy air.
Not funny.
I cannot give life on an apprentice's pay.

I have to learn to butcher.

Sharpened by Appetite

Moving slowly to not arouse suspicion, he scanned the space
drew a few short glares from some big males,
who looked away bored,
but measured his movements, timing the next glare
for a spot where he should have arrived.
Any misstep, hesitation, acceleration would elict a pounce.
They always saved energy for a pouncing.

He steadily continued as he located choice targets,
measured them trigonometrically,
tracked them,
analyzed for habits
teased out predictable vulnerabilities.

They stood laughing or shrieking in play
looked oblivious,
interested only in each other.

He wondered if they could be watching him
unmasking his intentions
relaying them in code to one another.

He would soon find out,
maybe get thrashed in the attempt.

He rechecked his exit strategy

readied to break his stride.

Looking Forward

Go forward into opaque, every moment of your life. Any fear is not
of darkness,
but of guessing.
Lack fear? It is only because of repetition. You might even get cocky,
except you recall a time before...

Go forward into opaque, with hope. You have found pleasure
so great you hardly noticed pain.
Eventually the pleasure is less.... again from repetition.
Still worth the pain?

Go forward into opaque, hopeless. If you do not,
you diminish.
If you still do not,
you end.

A fish darts from a cleft in the rock, hungry. It swims to the surface
and sees a struggling fly.
The fish eats, the fly ends.
If the fly is tied to a hook,
the fish ends.

A fish darts from a cleft in the rock. As it swims toward the surface,
it sees another fish. They mate.
The fish ends happy,
if fish can be happy.

Spring Waves

Spring breaks over me in waves:
the scent of rotting leaves
then sweet clematis,
a raven's guttural rattle
then chimes of the finch.

I, a plump brown spider
centered in my web of season
feel the ripple of arrival
the strum of struggle,
almost hear a tiny cry.

Winter fights to keep the throne,
but spring relentless
throws regiments of relief
at my frayed sufferance,
tiny shoots finally taking the field.

The fair Monarch's reign is short:
butterfly king,
I will watch you float through summer,
leave at the first crackle
of the fall campaign.

Numerology*

Outside were magpies;
a biting wind, warning call,
whiff of smoke
and a little more.

Inside was warm and bright,
the table cleared of dinner plates;
a wedge of pumpkin, berry, apple
and just a thin slice of cherry.

They had urged him;
think of population growth,
consider replacement reproduction
of slightly more children than two.
But he was stubborn,
had slightly more than three.

They all sat around the table,
a crease down its diameter
catching the white cloth;
candles radiated light
over the whole dining area.
The man circled the table,
served each child in turn,
faces animated at the sight;
to everyone his pie.

Into the Open, Exposed

1. Goldfish
You rise from the bottom, float among the duck weed,
your orange back
above the surface as you bask motionless
beneath the afternoon sun.

2. Brown Frog
You push out of your sunken nook,
the second stroke propels you onto a warm rock
where you bask motionless
beneath the late morning sun.

3. Primitive Human
You start off under a crescent moon
leave the safety of your dank cave
are halfway across the scrubland
stop to listen, ready to run hunched
when dawn breaks.

4. Human Idea
You will take it into the open,
this haunting thought
that seems to make sense in its nascent form
may sound half-baked when spoken aloud
might even bring you scorn and pain
until it dawns on someone else.

The Sigh

The old man-ape, aching in his joints
grunted whenever he moved
so he sat propped at the cave mouth
that overlooked the familiar valley
where his grandsons stalked game,
his granddaughters gathered stalks,
and as he thought,
just as we do today,
about how little
he had done with his life,
every day devoted to survival,
unable to make it better
for his offspring
who all chose to wear
hides on their feet,
like he had started doing
in his youth because one foot
got deeply cut,
but now he could not even
bend to put them on,
he let out a long sigh
that a great-granddaughter heard
and brought him a shell of water.

Oldest Person in the World

"I am the oldest person in the world."
"Now I am the oldest person in the world."
"Ha! Now I am the oldest person in the world."
"At last, I am the oldest person in the world."
"Sure it hurts, but I am the oldest person in the world"
"I try to keep moving and get a lot of rest."
"Ha! She said to keep moving and get a lot of rest.'
"Did anyone bring a fire extinguisher?"
"Good. One candle. That's about all I can blow out."
"Ha, his candle is out. Now I am the oldest person in the world."
 "Not easy tending goats on a Tibet mountain. Keeps you strong."
"I'm the oldest person in Japan, maybe the whole world."
 "I survived 26 angioplasties and 7 heart attacks."
"Never was sick a day in my life until I hit 95."
 "The trick is to have no one older alive."
"They won't let me drive anymore."
 "He didn't even get a recount."
"The life insurance is a bear."
 "It's not an elected office."
 "I plan to live forever."
"Okay, I can die now."
"Who are You?"
"Hot dog…"
"Where?"
"Arp"
"Pa?"
"Ha"
"Z"

Heritage

The wind blows dead limbs
from towering firs,
drops them in walkways,
hangs them on wires,
teetering
above my everyday path.

Squirrels dig pits in my lawn
by day, while at night
raccoons tunnel
under the house foundation
with thumps
and rhythmic scrapes.

The outside world is alive
with hazards,
everything in motion
shifting patterns
too numerous
to memorize.

I thank my predecessors
for senses
that guide me through
this maze,
realize I am but another
test organism
in this experiment
without a hypothesis.

Blossoms

Orchids never bloomed again
after store-bought petals dropped
and I pared the bare
stem that had borne
former flowers high
above broad leaves
splayed upon
the porous soil.

Decades of futility
finally ended
when I learned
those bare stems
do not shrivel completely
but bolster new buds,

flagpoles
from which future blossoms
can waft before my face
immodest in their promise
of earthy pleasures
whose purpose
of fertile seed
goes as unstated

as the taut blouse
over pre-teen
breast buddings
that first caught my notice
before I learned to think
upon intention
and consequence.

Borders

It borders on sanity,
our obsession with boundaries:
someone who used to be on our side
we now decide to dislike,
as if there were only winners and losers,
and we choose to sacrifice friendship
to support some temporary cause.

The harder choice,
to keep civility
throughout a conflict,
is mostly about trusting the judges,
someone to settle a tiff
    over that tree on the fence line,
someone to allocate funds
    to fix potholes in our lane,
someone to protect us.

Late in life, when some boundaries
seem less distinct,
our civility reflects how
we embrace our legacy,
worry less about next year's problems,
and allow someone else
    to have the babies, the big ideas

so we can be freed
to ponder
a game
of checkers,
if there really is
a higher judge
and if our body
can shrink
its borders
any further.

Echoes of Hard Knocks

All sorts of experiences bounce off the inside of my cranium,
an imperfect surface that distorts echoes
as they rebound toward my centers of judgment,
make me prone to miscalculation.

Lots of mundane encounters that started little waves
to lap with regularity upon the shores of motivation,
then just peter out,
allow me to be that guy everyone can count on,

but the occasional big impression keeps
rebounding, bounding, sounding
to add or subtract in contact
with echoes of other old traumas
to occasionally make me do bizarre things,
like write this poem.

Life Resume'

List of my tasks completed:
1) Magna Cum Lauda,
2) BS, MS, PhD, Post Doc, Managing Broker
3) Marriage, Phi Beta Children
4) Kappa Countless Crosswords.

Here is my real life resume':
1) "Don't get wise, beebee eyes.
Watch your lip, potato chip.
Understand, rubber band."

"I ain't afraid of you."

2) The moment I felt perfectly content
for no apparent reason,
sitting at the back of a bowling alley
with my old friend, Ray
wondering if this would be the only time
I would ever feel this way,
which so far, it has been.

3) The day I wore a kafiyah and told strangers
I was an Arab, and lied and lied and lied
just to see if I could keep it up and if I would like it,
but the lack of trust did not fit my self-image.

4) The day I pointed my camera at the young Orthodox Jew
who dived into a doorway just outside
the Mei-ah Sharim district of Jerusalem
after which a group leader scolded me, "For Shame,"
because I was amused that anyone would think a photograph
could capture their soul. Now 53 years later
I wonder if someone did lose their soul
how they would judge the value of keeping one.

5) The moment I realized I had changed
my own fate
when I had convinced Marty to go to the "Hillel Mixer"
where he met and married Linda
and I met no one,

except by the time Marty and Linda divorced
I had already married Cathy,
Linda's sister.

6) The night of snowflakes when I first knew love,
after dinner, with Cathy
at the bottom of the driveway,
the feeling
so different from
simple attraction or exploration.

7) The sight of the ear
which popped out at childbirth,
not a cleft-lip after all,
that closed the link in the chain
connecting me to those before and after.

8) The day my father forgave his father,
that "Son of a Gun," who probably was tough
because that was how fathers in immigrant families acted
when 2 of 12 children died young.
Forgiveness,
and then
my father
died within the week.

Cleaning the Toilet

Again I am cleaning the toilet,
as a foam sopped sponge
seeps into the sink
rinses away noticed detritus
until the porcelain properly shines.

It is a great necessity,
this cleaning of the toilet,
even if handed to hired help
or ignored until guests will come,
one cannot endure in a fouled nest.

Birds know this.
The mother alights, beaks gape,
a cricket is deposited,
a head retracts,
a cloaca is presented.
The mother takes the fecal sac in her bill,
flies away to deposit it
in a government sanctioned landfill,
or wherever will not give away
the location of her toilet's careful cleaning.

It Flows Down

It pours down from clouds
flows out of the hills,
from gutters drips loud
seeps soft off the sills

always goes downward
when left just to be,
glacier to barn yard
from sewer to sea.

Add force from the winds
or heat from the sun
sopping from napkins
or hot magma's run

then water can rise
in gravity's face
as new clouds comprise
and geysers take place.

Man, always eager
to harness raw strength
builds wheels with vigor
dams up rivers' length.

Feeling so clever
to run mills with nature
man forgets ever:
he's nature's creature

is even today
not smart as a tree.
Redwoods draw water
to high canopy

to make their own food
by using the sun
and add some more wood
when drawing is done.

Leap of the Ghazal

Eventually everyone will know all, no need for *alma mater*.
Every injury, disease cured, unending eons of living matter.

Atomic nuclei subdued, with ceaseless power in harness.
Energy for living beings, until growth no longer matters.

Time, as forward, will lose its meaning, nothing to await.
Slow or fast toward no end, arrives every form of matter.

Constants squared, their work done, will be only boring.
Everything then a constant, no motion will even matter.

If I were to merge with everything, no place left for God,
it'd be time to Big Bang myself apart, mind into matter.

If I Were to Pojack

If my religion permitted Christmas trees or
if decorated trees were really poems
each year I would select a new
evergreen that smelled of fir or spruce
whose branches and needles were unique
to display cardboard ornaments made
by my young brothers,
light-diffracting globes from Belgium gifted
by my spouse,
faded wooden houses enduring
from mother's childhood
and father's metal-shop fabrications.

If I were to pojack a structure upon
which to hang such treasured ornaments
I would select a prominent poem,
submerge it in peroxide to dissolve
away the great poet's display until
nothing remained but a lattice of veins,
like an autumn leaf on frozen soil.

But it is too late.
I have brought old plywood from my basement,
built a base to hold a stained wooden stud,
already drilled holes for dowel rods,
sawn them shorter to install ever higher until
a skeleton appears
and asks,
"Won't you please give me life
and if I might bother you further,
could you try and make me beautiful?"

No Complaints

I don't want to complain about the pain in my hip
a faithful joint that has carried me along forest edge
held me hunched among the mid-summer golden rod
to spy on a brown bunting carrying
a plump grasshopper to her nest, woven
waist-high between four upright stalks.

That same noble hip upheld the weight of a backpack
on Isle Royale, where numbers of wolves and moose
wax and wane like the sloshing of Lake Superior,
which sends the island river in a backwards flow
at regular intervals that can disorient
hikers who thought they had known
on which bank they traveled.

This hip held as I hoisted my children to watch
the Lake City Parade, where a float
with Hard Metal band members
decked in sharp trinkets
contrasted starkly with the softness of the clowns,
equally bizarre, except many toddlers are prone
to cry at the grotesque faces, bloated bodies of clowns.

The band float was banned the following year,
yet grown-up children still flocked to see them perform,
perhaps like the way kids play with miniature dinosaurs
eventually to marvel at huge spike-toothed skulls in the museum.

I gladly live with this soft ache in my hip
and maybe I will be ready when
it starts to get sharp.

Petroleum Rising Pantoum

Black glob breaks the surface
oozes up from oily depths
lurks among grass or sand
melts under the California sun

oozes up from oily depths
taints a beach with streaks of gray
melts under the California sun
sticks to soles of bare feet

taints a beach with streaks of gray
engulfed wolves, mired mammoths
sticks to soles of bare feet
sucked life beneath its surface

engulfed wolves, mired mammoths
stained skulls a telltale taupe
sucked life beneath its surface
releases bones from asphalt beds.

Sustaining Sestina

Plant your garden with care, dear friend
or face a rude abaganing
come and rake clods into loam
then turn up dirt until you drop
sweeten your acid soil with lime
muster de seeds, plant none too deep.

Roots start to grow into the deep
stems uncurling a leaf or frond
in early spring, depends on clime,
Mother Nature abeckoning
moistens the plantlets drop by drop
you witness miracles, loam

behold, tiny florets now loom,
and if you look into them deep
before they grow large and drop
petals that attract a bee friend
you perceive a new beginning
the start of a life so sublime

reminds of our rise from the slime
when we crawled naked and alone
on the shore of awakening
where self awareness now runs deep
and we learn how to trust a friend
to help harass our prey and drop

our normal guard and even drop
mating rivalry for a time
work without thought to help a friend
raise himself from the flooded loam
where he too sudden wades waist deep
risked more than he was bargaining

and we will not need a begging
will hold fast, not let him drop
for our humanity runs deep
when human life is on the line

we know we cannot live alone
need validation from a friend.

Observing plants to ponder life
dropped pretense and wish Shalom
to every deeply valued friend.

South Carolina…

t   ook most   of

a frac   tured
cen   tu   ry
a   nd a hal   f
t

o

s

t

e

m
rallying
'round the flag
of finite heritage

Set Table

The mouse almost makes it into the lawn,
is batted back onto the patio
as the kitten anticipates supper,
forces her prey into foreplay,
and like the dogs of Pavlov who begin
to drool pools at the ringing of a bell,
the kitten knows when hunger will be slaked,
imminent as a set table.

My dog recognizes the set table,
barks like each passersby is expected,
understands the odds are in his favor
that food will be dropped on the floor,
shamelessly snatches goodies from toddlers,
pinpoints a prospective patron
and begs by her seat with sad puppy eyes.

Our dogs and cats sense amazing detail
and bare the ability to predict
how a person will likely next react.
Since my pets also demonstrate emotions
of their own, I am left to wonder if,

like people, they can combine these two skills,
infuse emotion into prediction,
prophesy some upcoming commotion
with excitement or dread, appreciate
calm before a clamor, just as we do
when we see...

instruments perched upon a draped table...

empty sanctuary with prayer books
set neatly on every seat...

suitcases standing in an entry.

Appreciating the End

The winds wailed in his ears
numbed from the roar of twin Johnsons
that frothed water behind a boat
tossed to a choppy rhythm
of swells bearing froth of their own.

It was hard to fix on the shoreline
let alone on a single dock
hidden behind a breakwater
that lofts a pole and wind-frayed flag
to nearly reveal the way home.

He would not slow to check his path
for fear the storm would pull him under
so he sped before frigid clouds
glimpsing his target in instants
from crests of waves through parted spray.

Hopefully destined to reach shore
if not upon calm surface,
by some route above the waters,
he had heard there were
always storms
at the end, so
accepted the
choppy ride
as his
to
cherish.

Discovery...Of Sorts

Columbus discovered an America full of residents,
had named after him cities and a university.

Audubon discovered American bird colors,
had named after him a society and a warbler.

Peterson discovered American bird distinctions,
had named after him some field guides.

I discover a Western Tanager hop
near the water-flow by my patio.
How long it was there does not matter.
I share the excitement of early explorers.

"Endless Possibilities" a mosaic by Cathy Shiovitz
Photo by Tom Hefferan

5

RULES OF THE UNIVERSE

2015 - 2016

Sizing-Up the Universe*

Perspective is gone from my sense of size:

whether a man meets my gaze directly

peers down at me or raises up his eyes

matters no more than how the moon can shrink

in its nightly trek from the horizon

or outshine galaxies at endless heights

which I am told are still growing higher

while their inside pieces pull together

as if the whole universe is a ball field

wall-less and empty save for one plump coach

who is calling the few lagging fielders

to come home so a new game can commence.

Stationary

Patty had tried moving forward in time,
imagined her wedding glow,
the faces of sleeping infants,
a mellow stroll through old age,
but she always woke to the present
where she spent her life
slogging through a bog of insignificance
that caused her to slip backwards
into reprised sequences she valued
where even these moments were torn
by yammering relatives
or coworkers who wanted
to steal her stapler
or a comet,
so she strove to become stationary,
let events run past her
like a white Buick in the middle lane,
and except for attracting the occasional
piece of space dust,
she grew older undisturbed
with little hope of waking to a worthy thought,
until suddenly she found herself buried
standing up.

One Good Turn

Sometimes you just have to poke
the bug and see what happens.

Most of Patty was present on earth
attending to customers,
dispensing lattes, collecting money,
pocketing some pretty nice tips,

but a part of Patty's mind wandered
as she wondered if we were as alone
in the universe as she sometimes felt
at night in her studio apartment.

Surely she had lots of friends and family
back in her home town
and now when Patty heard their phone voices,
watched their photos and short videos

she could sense the warmth of affection,
almost feel their touch,
so she determined to think hard on a former classmate,
concentrate on remembered details of his face

while repeating over and over the words,
"I love you," "I love you,"
which greatly overstated her actual feelings
for this was a sort of experiment

that maybe was one reason three weeks later
he contacted her on-line
with a recent photo that appeared
far less blemished and more sincere.

Even so, Patty had little interest
in amorous pursuits, recalled
his uncontrolled personality that made
any real relationship impossible.

Instead, she strove to figure out how
distant bodies influence each other,

fingered the steaming cup
of coffee before her

and gave it one full turn.

Not Looking For Love*

Patty never looked for love,
but often was attracted
when a heavenly body
passed nearby.

She had endured hard lessons
from countless early clashes,
how others enhanced
themselves at her expense.

Even family members
still controlled her,
especially big sister around whom
major events revolved,

while her twin
constantly tugged at her world,
shamelessly taking rings
and other possessions.

Patty had experienced
the hell of being torn apart,
searing explosive reactions
of unsettled relationships,

so now she was just cooling down,
moving through her daily routine,
caring not the least
that she was traveling in circles.

Deep Roots of War

The last black hole was a messy eater,
popped star systems like cherry tomatoes,
X-rays streaming from the sides of its mouth,
sopped up later by the galactic
equivalent of a thick slice of potato bread.

No planet begged for mercy,
the black hole never justified its hunger
but like an angler fish, patiently waited,
attracted and devoured
nearly every morsel in the universe.

By the time Earth in turn was lost,
dissolved into particles and energy
neatly shrunk and stored,
gone were the battles over bones
between dogs
who had honored strength
while tolerating weakness,
and gone were all humans.

Yet a vestige remained deep within the black hole
where an infinitely small part
of Patty
was dusting, cleaning up, moving errant
sub-nuclear particles out of the head office,

and where Patty left
the particles of her coffee cup
next to one of the many triggers,
such as those that had set off
crowded rats
to attack each other,

when suddenly the cup
spun in a circle
and struck the
trigger which
caused the
black
hole
to explode into a universe reborn.

All Relatives*

Distant galaxies are   moving   away
like olives in a rising loaf of bread.

No worries.
You will keep loose contact
through a cousin olive
who encountered a traveler
or through a neighbor
who just returned from an exotic vacation.

Better to pay attention to our own galaxy
as it pulls together
still practicing hard
becoming better organized every day.

You might want to keep an eye on our solar system
where a newly suspected ninth planet
has been caught influencing
some far-out outliers,
and you wonder how a planet as big as Jupiter
can lurk unnoticed in billion mile shadows,
then pop out to steal Pluto's stash.

No worries.
It's probably not really a new ninth planet,
just a big cinder from the burned-out twin of the Sun
who helped string the dust between siblings
into a planetary archipelago
and now can't even earn a good obituary.

Perhaps appreciate that we are in a Golden Age
even though we eat our many-times-removed cousins
on slices of other many-times-removed cousins
and the future looks to stack
the entire population of earth
pressed against the walls of an elevator

and despite how difficult to digest,
we really are in a Golden Age,
where we can understand family
a lot of the time.
help each other endure hard times
and maybe even enjoy a steaming cup of coffee

that just mysteriously turned around in a circle.

Messing A-Rondeau

Patty thanked the night time sky
for sparkling kin so far and high
under which she sought a mate,
wondered when, as it grew late,
she would meet her destined guy.

It happened over cheese on pie,
he moved his hand to brush her thigh
on this merely their second date,
Patty thanked the night time sky.

He spoke of love, removed his tie,
she caught her breath and then a sigh,
she told him though he was her fate
the next few steps would have to wait,
and when he smiled, did not ask why,
Patty thanked the night time sky.

Anti-Water

Yesterday, Patty watched a tsunami
wash three floors up a condo.
Today she scorched herself
on latte machine steam.
Tomorrow she will see a hose
topple desperate protesters.

Yesterday Patty loosed her eggs before
hustling sperm in a pristine stream.
Today she serves it hot through filtered beans,
her pot fired by falling water.
Tomorrow she will milk it from Martian soil.

Yesterday Patty replied to a customer,
It makes no more sense
to be opposed to war
than to be opposed to water.
The goal is to harness them.

Today on a late summer afternoon
Patty strolls from the store in shorts
wades in the nearby Sound
senses lapping waves
of light and water.

Tomorrow she will surf
on waves of gravity.

Barry Steps Over the Line

Barry placed the leather encased tape recorder under a bush. He tied the bird ornament, blue with a black beak, on a branch a few feet above, pushed the "Play" button and quickly hid behind some cover. Ten yards away at the top of a tree, a singing bunting appeared then darted past the dummy bird to a bush nearby, intoning even while flying. Its song started to include emphatic buzzes between syllables as the bird dove again past the dummy, passing low to strike the tape recorder with its claws, its beak. In his notebook, Barry scored this episode a ten. It was the baseline song test of a real indigo bunting claiming territory. Now Barry tested his computer-generated song. It evoked a pretty strong response and he scored it a nine.

In the faculty lounge, Barry listened to his astronomer friend describe the new parabolic recorder, capable of receiving and bouncing signals into space. Excited, Barry followed him into the lab, watched him punch in a simple security code and input a signal to the new apparatus. *Indeed, I would be delighted to come back this evening and watch it in action.* And despite his friend calling in ill, Barry showed up alone, punched in the code, and attached two wires from his recorder head to the parabola's input. He pushed "Play" and sent his bird song pattern deep into space.

Moments later Patty awoke to ask herself aloud, *What the heck is that irritating noise?* She supposed they would send out a drone to investigate, which of course, they did.

After a few Earth minutes, Barry was looking out the lab window when suddenly the moon disappeared, as did the stars and planets. Trembling, he lunged toward the tape recorder and quickly pushed the "Off" button. A few seconds later, the shadow across the night sky moved on. Barry unhooked his wires, grabbed his recorder, quietly backed into the hall and closed the laboratory door.

Back home his hand still shook as he entered a score of seven.

Rules of the Universe: Food for Thought

Barry weighed his thoughts,
chewed them over carefully.
He could regurgitate facts, but
was fascinated by laws behind them.
As they were hard to digest, he broke
them into pieces small enough to absorb.
When processed, he had no excess to waste.
He had mentally metabolized everything
in the universe, arriving at the following conclusions:

1) All matter, energy and forces in the universe always remain in behavioral relationships with each other and disparate parts of themselves.

2) Rules of these relationships constantly develop variants some of which, tested over increasing time and space, remain relevant.

Satisfied that he had unified everything from
The Big Bang to super-organism societies,
Barry softly belched
and slipped into an
after dinner
snooze.

Notes

Associations

This poem was inspired by my model for how certain bird species can decode and learn their songs, distinguishing them from all other nearby singing birds. I measured recordings of songs that were sound spectragraphed, and played doctored songs to see if they elicited territorial defense behavior. In one set of playback songs, sound was removed at regular intervals and replaced by silence. My findings suggested that intervals of about 9 milliseconds were involved in species recognition by the indigo bunting.

To understand my model, let's first imagine you are standing in a bathtub surrounded by 4 inch tiles. You put your index finger and pinkie of one hand on a horizontal grout line between the tiles. You then move your hand to the right and encounter vertical grout lines. If your two fingers are separated by exactly the width of a tile, they will encounter the vertical grout lines at exactly the same time. Any closer between them and they will never simultaneously encounter a vertical grout line.

This is the idea of a "flicker frequency," proposed by an earlier researcher. That is, if the distance between your two fingers is a time period, then the bird would need to hear two sounds separated by an exact time period, which I call a "beat."

Let's add a level of complexity. You go to a piano and move one finger left, down the (scale) keys, then right, up the keys. Let's say that each key is a time period of one beat. My model suggests the birds count time periods that are digital (here, literally!). They would count the number of keys (amount of time) that the notes go down, then the number up. This is a timing system that is so simple that a young bird could conceivably learn by it.

Let's add another level of complexity. You play the piano with your right hand, stretching it so your thumb is on middle C and your pinkie is on C one octave higher. You maintain that distance between the two fingers as you move left down the scale. Any other distance does not sound the same. We recognize a simultaneous exact octave, and I suggest that a recognizable beat-separated pitch increment may exist in birds.

I could add other levels of complexity, such as the addition of vibratos and buzzes, but if you have followed me this far, I am happy if you appreciate the simplicity of this model.

A more complete control system model for vertebrate behavior, can be found in my essay "Robots, Bird Song and Dirty Dancing," in the website for this book at rulesoftheuniverse.com.

Yo-Yo
Web published by Kota Press.

Kitchen Shopping
This tone poem has been a successful presentation piece that derived from recordings of the song of the indigo bunting, *Passerina cyanea*, at one-quarter speed. It's rhythmic source was recognized only after it was composed.

Chicken Scratch for Henry
Successful presentation piece as reader devolves into a chicken. Name unrelated to Uncle Henry.

Uncle Henry
Henry Krystal MD. 1925-2015   New York Times Obituary, 10/14/15.

Bargain
Published in Drash: A Northwest Mosaic.

From Whence I Came
(Source: Personal communication with Pearl Shiovitz LeVine, Louis Shiovitz and Harry Shiovitz; Family Tree as developed by Pearl Shiovitz LeVine, Louis Shiovitz, Donald LeVine, and Nathan Shiovitz).

Location of the Zborofsky family home is known only as in the Ukraine. Jacob's path, means, and condition of escape are conjecture. Escapees were often given the name of the rabbi in a destination town.

Beard color is apparently passed maternally, but red is common enough in the family to use it for "poetic color."
Knee cartilage damage has appeared in all four of Louis' sons: Bill, Ken, Jim, and Tom.

Jacob was so much taller than Devorah that their grandchildren sometimes referred to them, discretely, as "Mutt and Jeff."

Jacob's mother's name was Chia(h). It is unknown whether she was living at the time of Jacob's escape. Jacob's brother was Abraham, and his sister was Laka.

Devorah's mother was also Chia. Devorah had four step-siblings from her father Borah's (Boruch?) earlier marriage to Rose. It is poetic conjecture that her father and step-sister Getchel died at the hands of the Cossacks.

The spelling of Hirlau in a 1911 map was later changed to Harlau. The village still exists today.

The nickname Max is the Americanized version of his given name, Isaiah Mordecai. Isaiah is likely after his grandfather, the Shia of the original name Shiovitz. The name of sister Rose is Americanized from the Yiddish, Raisel Laya. Devorah is Americanized Hebrew for Deborah, and the Yiddish, Dora.

Max was the second oldest sibling after Rose. The others were Fannie, Henry, Lena, and Ida. The Rothschilds funded the flight of 18 year old Jews from Romania to Canada. Rose preceded Max to Detroit, with her husband and child. She arrived via Liverpool, England, by boat to Halifax, Nova Scotia or St. John, New Brunswick, then by train to New York City. They stayed in tenements for six weeks, then were called by Jewish Social Services, along with 16 other families to come to Detroit to work in the factories (source: her grandson).

Bad Axe is located near the thumb of Michigan. The winters there are extremely frigid. The two young sons were buried in Detroit.

Max continued his hauling business, mostly of store fixtures, and eventually opened a store, "Avon Store Fixtures," which was supposed to be "A-1," but his heavy accent misdirected the sign painter.

Louis' maternal grandmother was also named Devorah and also short. In fact she, Devorah Guttmann Shear, was called "Little Bubbe" (Little Grandma), and lived at the family home for about 20 years after Devorah Shiovitz passed away in the early 1920s. Devorah Shiovitz was apparently illiterate and very quiet, but had an artistic bent. Devorah Guttmann Shear's family had a history of much more education than Jacob or Devorah Shiovitzs' families, and included many rebs (educated laymen) and rabbis, even to the renowned Vilna Gaon. Devorah Shear passed away in 1945.

Prophet Loss Statements
Published in Drash: A Northwest Mosaic.

Overjoyed
First line inspired from Ted Kooser, *Old Cemetery*.

Silent Travelers in a Bubble Chamber
Bubble chamber contains supersaturated solution that turns to small bubbles along a path that a subatomic particle has travelled.

Like Eagles Soar
Published in Drash: A Northwest Mosaic.

Winged Warriors
Published in Drash: A Northwest Mosaic.

Numerology
A numerical puzzle for you to figure out.

Sizing-Up the Universe
While the universe may expand forever, I prefer to think of it like the child's toy of a red ball attached to a paddle by a rubber band.
Forces eventually slow the outgoing ball and draw it back to the paddle. Even an object blown apart by TNT might not remain forever so disorganized. Its components may break down and be recycled by nature. The sun is expected to eventually draw in the planets, and/or the Milky Way's black hole to draw in its star systems.

Not Looking For Love
Intended to be interpreted on two different levels.

All Relatives

Logic for black holes as highly organized: From Big Bang singularity, matter and energy move out in array of disorganization. From there many elements organize into particles, planets, stars, galaxies, life, etc.. Black holes are expected to be highly dense relative to bodies they ingest.

Publications

Shiovitz, K.A., Thompson, W.L., 1970. Geographic variation in song composition of the indigo bunting, *Passerina cyanea*. Anim. Behav. 18, 151-158.

Thompson, W.L., Shiovitz, K.A., 1974. Song of the Bunting. Nat. Hist. 83 (8), 46-51.

Shiovitz, K.A., 1975. The process of species-specific song recognition by the indigo bunting, *Passerina cyanea*, and its relationship to the organization of avian acoustical behavior. Behav. 55, 128-179.

Shiovitz, K.A., Lemon, R.E., 1980. Species identification of song by indigo buntings as determined by responses to computer generated sounds. Behav. 74, 167-199.

Shiovitz, K., 2007. Bargain. Drash: NW Mosaic 1, 42

Shiovitz, K., 2008. Prophet Loss Statements. Drash: NW Mosaic 2, 80.

Shiovitz, K., 2011. Like Eagles Soar. Drash: NW Mosaic 5, 21.

Shiovitz, K., 2013. Winged Warriors. Drash: NW Mosaic 7, 13.

Web Publications

http://kotapress.com/journal/Archive/journal_issue4/journal16.htm

http://itsaboutimewriters.homestead.com/ShiovitzBirdSong.html

Acknowledgements

This book is dedicated with love to my wife, Cathy, for many reasons including that I no longer know where one of us ends and the other begins. Her contributions have been artistic, intellectual, emotional, and practical. Our children, Dan and Stacey, are far more clever than us. They anchor the web that upholds us, supported also by their spouses, children, in-laws, my brothers Bill, Jim, Tom, and Cathy's sisters Linda and Julie and their families, and our cousins, aunts and uncles. While I am not listing every name here, their loving support has been endless, gracious, and so much appreciated.

Thanks are given in loving memory of my parents, Dr. Louis and Belleen Shiovitz, who led by example and occasional stronger methods, Cathy's wonderful mother, Dr. Helen Sherman and sister Amy Sherman. To Ed Sherman, Cathy's step father who is still living, thanks are given for support and many discussions about art and life. Of our many deceased loving aunts and uncles, special mention is given to Dr. Henry Krystal, who gave example, counsel and early appreciation of the world of nature and to his very much alively wife, Aunt Esther.

Many teachers have contributed to my ability to think and write. Foremost is my doctoral advisor, Dr. William Lay Thompson, who remains a dear friend. His wife Retta, has always been a support. My post-doctoral advisor, Dr. Robert E. Lemon, truly enriched my life. I thank the members of my doctoral committee. I also appreciate the team that taught Enriched English at Mumford High School, and my creative writing teacher at The University of Michigan, whose name I should have remembered.

Many colleagues contributed to my intellectual growth and factual knowledge. Dr. Orin Gelderloos and Dr. David Sokoloff, then at The University of Michigan, Dearborn, deserve special mention and remain friends. Their Matter, Energy, and Life course which I helped team-teach, remains an inspiration and source of interdisciplinary thought. Several fellow students and faculty at Wayne State University and McGill University have influenced my life and thought.

Rabbis have inspired my intellectual and behavioral life, through Torah discussions, leadership opportunities, and personal example. Jonathan and Beth Singer, Norman Hirsh, Ruth Zlotnick, Jason

Levine, the late Morris Adler and Reuven Frankel, are all treasured influences. Cantorial soloist and poetry journal editor, Wendy Marcus, has been a multifaceted influence on my temperament, thought and delivery of the spoken word.

Members of The PoetsTable writing group, which has met semi-monthly for decades have been an invaluable part of my development as a poet and we have grown close. Many of my poems, headed for failure, were rescued by their comments. Their honest reactions and suggestions are from poets whose own work I greatly respect. Of recent they included Murray Gordon, Dr. Len Tews, Nancy Dahlberg, Nan Hardy, Rodney Williams, Don Kentop, Cathy Ross, Carol Shaw, Laura Snyder, and Pieter Zilinsky. Murray and Len have shared personal philosophies that strongly influenced the stated "Rules." J. Glenn and Barbara Evans have much influenced my thought and supported my early poetic growth, both personally and through Poets-West. Esther Altshul Helfgott kindly gave exposure to my poetry and thought through her "Its About Time" venue, as did Red Sky Poetry Theater.

I am blessed with good friends, with whom I can safely check my intellectual and emotional well-being, philosophize, play, and enjoy a beer or a full blown feast. Dr. Ray Silverman and Dr. G. Mike Schneider have supported us immensely, as have their wives, Alice and Ruth Ann. Curt Colbert, Barbara Sharkey, Les Beletsky, and spouses have been exemplary through their publications and friendship. Byron Schenkman shared some of his extensive classical music knowledge, for which I am extremely grateful. Thanks to Linda Freyd for tracking down some photographs of Camp Kesher. Tom and Brigitte Hefferan always request a poem or two at dinners where we can count on a calligrapher guest artist to be present. Tom teaches photography as a passion, and I thank him deeply for inspiration and some photographs in this book.

Although not individually named here, there are other dear friends I wish to thank for their input into my life that is reflected in this book. They include widely scattered old friends, local Seattle area friends, and group members of: the late Bruce Kort's family, Friends of Michelle, TBA Torah Study, RPC, Minyan, our Chavurah, Art Feinglass and the Seattle Jewish Theater Company, leadership of Cathy's calligraphy guild, my philosophy lunch friends, poetry friends, and members of the Northgate office of Windermere Real Estate.

Stacey and Dan host "How well do you know Ken Shiovitz?" on occasion of his 70th birthday.
Photo by Tom Hefferan

Testimonials Continued

"Shiovitz's book begins like a stroll in the park, and ends with the reader strapped to a rocket cruising the stars; what a journey! "

Donald Kentop
poet author
of *Frozen by Fire*

"I am proud to be associated with Ken Shiovitz."

Carol Sage Silverstein
actor
at Seattle SJTC, Book-it-Repertory, Studio4 and Actors Equity

"Ken Shiovitz's poetry is always accessible, but rarely predictable -- his poetry is fun, while also being quite thought-provoking."

Curtis Colbert
author
of the Jake Rossiter mystery series, coauthor of the Waverly Curtis Chihuahua series including *The Chihuahua Always Sniffs Twice*

"A biologist's curiosity, a philosopher's conundrums, a poet's lens… a gem of a book! "

Barbara Brunk Sharkey
author
of two books including
Counselor Stories